Act and the Actor

Other books by Harold Rosenberg from Chicago

The Tradition of the New
The Anxious Object
Artworks and Packages
The De-definition of Art
Art on the Edge

Act and the Actor
Making the Self
Harold Rosenberg

The University of Chicago Press
Chicago and London

The University of Chicago Press, Chicago 60637
The University of Chicago Press, Ltd., London

90 89 88 87 86 85 84 83 1 2 3 4 5

Library of Congress Cataloging in Publication Data

Rosenberg, Harold.
  Act and the actor.

  Originally published: New York: World Pub.
Co., 1970. (Perspectives in humanism)
  Includes index.
  I. Title. II. Series.
[AC8.R62 1983]   126   82-25100
ISBN 0-226-72675-4 (pbk.)

Contents

Preface

The unity of this book is self-generated, rather than imposed through pursuing a preconceived theme. Regardless of what I was writing about in a period of more than twenty years, I found myself uncovering parts of the same motif. Lacking a program, I was able to rely on an obsession. In reflections on Oedipus and Kierkegaard, *Hamlet*, Marx, Dostoyevsky, Sartre, the trial of Eichmann, the matter that came to the surface, like an image revealed in a rubbing, was that of the identity of an actor, individual or collective, sham or genuine, forming itself through acts. Whether this theme is as pervasive as it has seemed to me, who can say? It emerged, I am convinced, out of the subjects themselves—not because it was projected by my angle of vision or by anything resembling a "method," but because it was, quite literally, *there.*

In sum, what is offered here is not a theory but a series of explorations, not an analysis of a literary, psychiatric, political or religious problem but clarifications of dramatic fictions within real and imagined situations. Action and acting are semi-illusory phenomena; they include not only the actors' hallucinations of mistaken identity but the inherent misapprehensions of their audiences. Every act involves a seepage of poetry into practical life. This mixture can be grasped only through concrete cases. The result is an exhibit of related thought events, rather than a system of interpretation.

As to the pertinence of a terminology derived, more or less spontaneously, from the alloy of theater and fact sampled in these pages, it is only necessary to glance at the politics of illusion dominant throughout the world. The following is from some remarks I included in the *Partisan Review* symposium on "What's Happening to America," conducted during the Johnson Administration:

The United States today is governed by professional illusionists. Not only are officials elected through campaigns of image-building based on fiction and caricature, but once in office their actions are decided not by anticipating consequences to the nation and/or humanity but by the kind of image those actions will enable them to present to the public. Washington acts by putting on an act. The same is true of every state capitol and city hall. With sheriffs behaving like movie actors, movie actors aspire to the highest offices.

Politics increasingly takes on the forms of mass culture, in which the picture of a thing, or the publicity about it, achieves precedence over the thing itself, since the latter is seen by considerably fewer people. . . . Events are contrived out of the whole cloth in order to provide occasions for actions or statements of policy. Events are made to happen for the sake of words, instead of words being used to give an account of events. History has been turned inside out; writing it takes place in advance of its occurrence, and every statesman is an author in embryo.

As to the aims of these actors, the performance itself is their highest aim, since it is their evidence of being alive.

Perhaps the best that modern society can hope for is an improvement in style.

HAROLD ROSENBERG

East Hampton, N. Y.
July, 1969

Act and the Actor

1

The Diminished Act

Wrote Valéry: "An act, originating in the psychic and physiological condition of some individual, is certainly a series of very complex transformations of which we have as yet no idea, no model." The Greeks, Valéry might have been thinking, did have a "model." In classical tragedy, as King Claudius said of heaven, an action "lies in its true nature." It occurs in the context of a plot which establishes its beginning, its middle and its end. In the Greek dramatic format, the act of the hero is set in motion by another act, instigated, ultimately, by a god or the Fates (e.g., the exposure of Oedipus), and the act is concluded by the decree of the god who descends on the stage. In sum, the hero's act is sandwiched between two divine actions—it is the visible portion of the hero's life, the scenario of which was conceived before he was born. Since he is playing a part laid out for him in advance, his act is also an acting. Man is a performing artist, the artist an imitator of the inventions (plots) of the gods. The primary human obligation is to play one's part well, that is, with dignified resignation, as other actors (Creon in

Oedipus Rex, the friends in the Book of Job) do not hesitate to remind the hero.

In our time *whole* acts are considered as belonging to epochs of myth. It is in the fabulous universe of timeless recurrence that acts exists in their entirety, while the human actor is still pecking away at the segments exposed in time. In the world of nature an act has neither beginning nor end. Composed of constantly changing combinations of human decision and physical energy, it is essentially hybrid, transitory and fragmentary—hence indefinable.

On the other hand, we have no end of models of human *behavior.* The intellect of our time is cluttered with patterns of the inner and outer motions of individuals. Each of the sciences of man—psychiatry, sociology, history, cultural anthropology, demography—presents an actor moved by systematically interrelated compulsions. In these structures the act of an individual begins not in a preceding act but in the operations of a process; and it ends by returning to that process. The perpetual-motion machine of psychic metamorphosis constructed by Freud converts instinctual impulses into decisions and gestures, and these in turn are transformed in the unconscious into new appetites. The sex *act* is a popping of energy generated in a sex *field.* In the Marxian model, socioeconomic changes provoke drives in social classes which are transmitted to individuals, and the resulting actions flow back into the social apparatus and cause readjustments in it. In these systems the act of an individual merges into movements of nature and history, into a measureless complex of organic and mechanical transformations.

Thus the character of the human act has become essentially ambiguous. Except in the formulas of absolute determinists, it has not been totally dissolved, but it is encroached upon at both ends—in its inception and its consequences, it melds into *events*. *A* performs act *X* as a reflex to stimuli in and around him; as a result, *Y* and *Z* occur automatically. Eichmann joins the Nazis because of conditions in post-World War I Germany, his relations with his parents, the de-individualization of Industrial Man. Having become an SS man, he is a "cog in the wheel" and his signing extermination orders follows as a matter of course. At his trial in Jerusalem, he tries to arouse sympathy by denying his power of choice, thus dissolving his actions into events of European history. Eichmann was prepared to confess what he had done, so long as he reserved the privilege of objectifying his deeds by treating them as if they had taken place without him. His world audience recognized that they too did things because they "had to," and that through persisting in the doing, men became exteriorized into "the clerk," "the policeman," "the man from underground." Each system of behavioral interpretation weighed upon a different scale the residue of action that belonged exclusively to Eichmann. The magnitude of causes and effects concentrated in initialing memoranda which consigned hundreds of thousands to the gas chambers placed the actor himself in a microscopic perspective—as if he were a mosquito responsible for a malaria epidemic. In *Crime and Punishment* Dostoyevsky conjectured that a crime that is large enough—Napoleon's total of slain, in contrast to Raskolnikov's—overwhelms the concept of guilt by taking on the character of a natural catastrophe. Blended into world events, the acts of Eichmann tended to shrink into a mere nuance of personality ("If he hadn't done the job, someone else would"). In the Soviets under Stalin, on the other hand, a huge calamity—a decline in food production, the collapse of a superdam—was presumed to be the effect of a criminal act, and persons were chosen to confess that they were guilty of it. Thus in the absence of a firm notion of an act, determinism can result both in a belief in "innocent" agents of evil and in individual responsibility for morally neutral events and "acts of God."

In the modern consciousness the human act, if it exists at all, is suspended at the intersection of numerous impersonal processes, some still unlabeled. To act is to locate oneself in a middle. The individual is aware that he has begun, but not where the beginning took place. He is aware, too, that the termination of his action is not in sight —"If it were done when 'tis done," he sighs like Macbeth. With its constantly fluctuating dimensions and its transitions between the accidental, the imaginary and the objectively determined, the act, whether of mass murder, philanthropy or creation, is the outstanding riddle of the twentieth century.

An intuition of the indeterminacy of the act underlies all advanced forms in art and social relations. The composition of a painting is thought of as an endless experiment, or as accomplished instantaneously by a fling of paint. Marriages take into account conditions for divorce. The Futurists coordinate art with the movements of crowds and racing cars, and the Constructivists with the rationale of industrial production. In art and politics an act is conceived as synonymous with a "happening," and the history of art is written as if works evolved out of one another without the intervention of artists. The happening as an art form finds its source in Action painting, though the emphasis of happenings on group improvisation, chance and play is antithetical to action as a medium of willed change. The confusion regarding action leads to the notion of the pure, or "gratuitous" act, that is, an act purged of motive, hence of inner or external coercion and of the possibility of being shared. Yet in divorcing itself from its source in the actor, the gratuitous act also becomes a kind of happening —and André Gide, the originator of the term, moved on in *The Counterfeiters* to the notion that the true novel must be improvised out of events that take place independently of the intentions of the actors, and that it can have no ending any more than events do. The condition of the actor acted on by his act is well described in the following passage from *Camden's Eyes,* a recent novel by Austin Wright: "this was something that had already been started, something happening to him, not a decision." Looking back a century, one finds the self-motivated act evoked by Dostoyevsky in the *A Raw Youth:* "I shouted that at the time unintentionally, I did not know a second before that I should say it: it shouted itself . . . Yes, crime was hovering about me that night, and only by chance was not committed." In *Crime and Punishment,* the crime *was* committed—also "by chance." Or did the crime commit itself using Raskolnikov as its tool?

By the logic of *The Counterfeiters,* a real person, as distinguished from a character in a romance or farce, lives through episodes but does not live through a resolution of them. Similarly, in Kafka's *The Castle* occurrences are so shrouded in half-hidden processes that the impossibility of ending the tale becomes its primary philosophical point. And in Kafka's *Amerika* a final chapter set apart from the narrative brings the sequence of happenings governed by coincidence and chance meetings to a halt in a paradise where the future turns back to retrieve the past.

The circular structure of Joyce's *Finnegans Wake* is another demonstration of the collapse of the dynamism of the act and its replacement by rhythms of organic process. Not only do end and beginning flow together in the river of prose that keeps returning upon itself, the microscopic metamorphosis of episodes is so rapid and continuous that the identities of the protagonists disintegrate, and potential acts exhaust their force in reshapings of language and minor physiological disturbances (e.g., gas pains). The model of *Finnegan* is Hamlet unpacking his heart with words, an act comparable to prayer—which Kierkegaard considered to be "the true form of the comic" (since its only outward manifestation is a movement of the lips) and which the priest Eli in the Old Testament mistook for drunkenness. Joyce's translation of human existence into a divine-comic rumination, in which Harold is Humphrey or Earwicker or Everybody, fulfills his conception, stated in *Ulysses,* of literature as an "epiphany" that lifts the psyche above the conflicts of drama and epic. Here, the abnegation of action is total. "For every man," said Hamlet, "hath business and desire, such as it is;—and for mine own part, look you, I'll go pray."

While Joyce cancels action through absorbing individual consciousness into the rhythms of universal metamorphosis, Joyce's disciple, Beckett, slows down action to an interminable crawl ("Tomorrow and tomorrow and tomorrow") which, as in Zeno's demonstration, is the logical equivalent of motionlessness. Thus life in Beckett's writings is a timeless waiting, which is another aspect of prayer. Instead of spiraling like *Finnegan* into rapturous verbal releases, *Waiting for Godot* achieves a state of enchained marking time, relieved by occasional rhetorical discharges. The subject of *Godot,* whether the waiting is for God or for death, is unimportant: the content of the work is its form—the chatter, the fits and starts, the moping back and forth, the return of the end to the beginning. Logically, the curtain should never fall; it does so only because of the practical necessity of clearing the theater of invertebrates, in order to make room for the next swarm of crawlers who will be hypnotized into postures of piety. The audience experiences a purge of its restless will to act through an exasperated waiting for the end of the play, and this end never arrives in action but only in time. The spectator has, in a word, been lured into an "endgame," the point of which is to maintain a semblance of motion while being aware of the impossibility of ever getting out of his seat.

In Action painting the pressing issue for artists was: When is a painting finished? Answer: At exactly the end of the artist's lifetime. Acting to the end, instead of waiting for the end. In both acting and waiting, there is no outcome, no conclusion, except the condition itself. For an artist to choose acting is, however, more intellectually apt than to choose waiting, since to create a work one must act, though waiting may be part of it, too. This rule applies to Beckett himself, poet of the hung-up and the slow shuffle. If life were only waiting (for a long time Beckett did wait) there would be no *Waiting for Godot.* Thus Beckett proposes one law (hopelessness) for the audience, another for himself, the artist. Like all theories of a creative elite, this carries an odor of priestly privilege, and there is something didactic about Beckett's helplessness. In outlook he is removed from Joyce, who affirms creation as the native condition of man, even in the act of making of "sweet religion a rhapsody of words"—and Joyce's attitude is shared by the Action painters in their search for epiphany or self-transcendence through the act of composition.

The Action painters and Beckett have responded, though in different ways, to the same predicament: that in our time the human act is veined with currents of inertia and lacks shape and measure. As a result, even the most elementary forms—the rectangular shape of the canvas and the dimensions suggested by its future place on a wall; the three-act play that resolves a situation in an evening—appear as arbitrary limits. In order to be faithful to reality, compositional space and time are replaced by quantities of feet and minutes: mini plays and daylong happenings, shaped and wall-size canvases. With external dimensions deprived of significance, the crucial dimension for the artist is the duration of the act of creation. How long can he sustain his act as an act, before it is caught in the tide of some ongoing process, psychological, historical, aesthetic? The issue of the duration of the creative act has given rise to instantaneous art, automatism, "process" art, collective art (e.g., chain poems and drawings). In radical politics, the time stretch of the creative is at the center of the struggle between advocates of mass spontaneity and centralized direction.

Characterizing a work by the duration of the experience out of which it arises is by no means confined to action painting. "It's not even a beginning," said Giacometti in a *Godot*-ish vein about a portrait on which he had been working for days, "and never will be." In an interview a few years ago, Peter Weiss, author of *Marat/Sade,* repeated the theme of the dimensionless work. "The form of the book," he said about his novel, *Gesprach der Drei Gehenden,* "is such that it can never be brought to an end. It lies in the nature of the book that it can never be anything but a fragment because it is an interior monologue and an interior monologue goes on as long as one lives." But an external event is a "fragment," too, and Weiss's historical drama, *Marat/Sade,* does not end either. Threatened throughout with immediate termination by Coulmier, director of the asylum where Sade's play was given, the performance is finally called off by the actor-stage manager, and the cast of "lunatics" and the people in the theater are left facing each other. Unable to determine the scale of a segment of history, in this instance the assassination of Marat, Weiss has transposed the incident into the double mirror of a theatrical performance that reenacts a theatrical performance. Twice removed into fiction, the historical event becomes as completely "interior" as an interval of memory and equally subject to intellectual tampering—it was reported that Weiss offered a different interpretation of the play each time it was produced. The playwright thus underlines our (and his) ignorance of the nature of the act and surrenders any pretense of grasping its reality.

Traditionally, of course, the imitation of action is the substance of drama, as color is of painting, sound of music. Without an intuition of the act, drama turns into something else—spectacle, fairy tale, visual teaching aid. That something is missing in the theater has been a popular topic since the last century, when the multiplication of scientific interpretations began to erode the human act. Tied to its audiences, however, for whom the formulas of psychology, sociology and political ideologies had become realities of daily life, twentieth-century drama has rarely troubled to speculate about the present status of the act. Dramatic literature, including the novel and the film, has usually contented itself with variations upon the behavior of abstract types brought into being by concepts of individual and group responses. The predetermined reflexes of classified neurotics, or of personifications of class or occupation, have been adapted to fit modifications of conventional plot structures. Edward Albee, Tennessee Williams, Arthur Miller are examples of playwrights who have set their dial permanently at the psychopathology of daily life. In fables dealing with material of this sort, the form of the act is mechanically predetermined, and "life" is injected into the machinery of events through poetic rhetoric and the temperament of the actors—to grasp their parts the latter consult not the play and their lines but their therapists. In effect, the play is a "natural" occasion, an opportunity for acting out a series of happenings in different categories—a seduction, a mental breakdown, a siege of domestic nagging. Beginning in a personal or social disorder, the drama attains its curtain through an appeal to a moral, social or psychological "solution" (e.g., love) in which no one believes.

Dramas of process in this vein use the theater as a lecture platform to demonstrate how life is lived for us. By contrast, the theater of the non-act, that of Brecht, Beckett, Ionesco and other modernists, is the serious dramatic art of this time, in that it has identified the act as the substance of theater and grappled with the implications of getting along without it. Born in Pirandello's discovery that the theater has nothing to base itself on but theater copied by life, it has, through Beckett's limp mutterers, Brecht's alienated abstractions, Weiss's lunatic mimics, Ionesco's animated things, and the nobodies of the happenings, posed in negative terms the interdependence of action and individuality shown forth in the soluble identities of *Finnegan*. The formula reached has been: no act, no actor; or $0 = 0$ —which, at any rate, has a certain nobility.

It seems likely that the poets of anti-drama have gone too far (it is the business of art to go too far) in surrendering the individual to the void of events. Individual acts have diminished, but they have not totally disappeared. If nothing else, there remains the act of writing plays and novels about inaction, in sum, the act of creation. In this act, a beginning is marked off, and energies are set into motion— the absence of these energies will identify the end of the act.

Lacking a better "model" of the act, it was to the anatomy of creation in art that Valéry turned. To this study he devoted fifty years (to the mystification of critics who could not comprehend why a poet should write so much about writing poetry). Valéry's model creator was fashioned out of the mental stance of Leonardo, Descartes, Mallarmé; and he analyzed the psychic condition of twentieth-century Europe in order to estimate the chances of survival of his synthetic performer. Granted that the practice of an artist or philosopher cannot attain the wholeness of the act of the dramatic hero in its context of myth, the composition of a work of art does contain a point of beginning and an interval of choice—that is to say, it contains the outline of a free act. No wonder that the artist has become the riddle of philosophers, psychiatrists and theologians, and the envy of men of affairs, in this age of process.

2

The Pathos of the Proletariat

"And he himself must speak through [the mask] saying thus . . . 'If you think I come hither as a lion, it were pity of my life: no I am no such thing: I am a man as other men are:'—and there, indeed, let him name his name, and tell them plainly he is Snug the joiner."

A Midsummer Night's Dream

"The working class is either revolutionary or it is nothing."

KARL MARX

I

The hero of Marx's drama of history is, of course, the proletariat. It is the action of this "character" that is to resolve the tragic conflict and introduce the quiet order of desired happenings. To be sure, there would still be conflicts under communism; the clash of individuals affirming themselves against one another and against society would not cease. But the antagonisms of that order would not be bloody struggles like those bred in the imagination of dramatic poets. Conflicts rather as among the themes in the mind of the philosopher, stirring his thought and enriching it. Through the socialist revolution, the world of Aeschylus and Shakespeare, whom Marx reread each year, would rise to the world of Hegel, the teacher whom he refused to abandon.

Who is this actor who was to "realize philosophy," as Macbeth his ambition or Orestes his revenge? And who, by causing events to take on the transparency of thought, was to release mankind from the opacity of material needs— and from the excessive act, the hypnosis of the past, the estrangement of men from themselves and others?

The hero of history was to be a social class, a particular species of collective person. What is a "class"? In *The German Ideology*, Marx describes a class in general terms. As distinguished from other unions, "there exists," says he, "a materialistic connection of men with one another." The class differs from the cult or the nation in being born out of direct physical relationships among individuals and between them and the things they need in order to live.

Arising out of these vital relations, Marx goes on to explain, the class is dedicated to affirming itself in the material world. It is formed for combat, "to carry on a common battle against another class." It is thus an active social entity; the class is more than a mere collection of human beings. Its principle of activity separates it from its individual members. Like an army, "the class in its turn achieves an independent existence over against the individuals" who compose it. An aggressive entity, it stands apart from persons and forces them into the orbit of its own actions.

For Marx the class has character and an historical physiognomy; the individual, independently of class, has neither. The material relations in which individuals have existed until now have never permitted the human being to be himself. His needs of subsistence and the menace of others have fused him to his class; to the extent that he is thus joined, he is, says Marx, an "abstract individual." The class "subsumes" him under itself and "subjects him to all kinds of ideas, etc." The class is identical with that in the life of the individual that prevents him from being an individual. It is the non-self of the person and of others in the same situation taking on positive features, as when the empty space between two objects in a painting forms the outline of a figure. The class is inescapably present to the individual as another self—it is the reality of his unreality.*

History for Marx is the rise, struggle and decline of such separated non-human entities. It is neither the history of individuals nor the history of ideas.

This [materialistic] connection is ever taking on new forms, and thus presents a "history" independently of any political or religious nonsense that would hold men together on its own.

Precisely because it represents the actions of the extra-human classes must history be brought to an end, if the individual is to be freed into full being. And for the same reason, only the class acting as "character" in the drama of history can perform the acts necessary to terminate it.

From *The German Ideology* we derive only the most general notions about the proletariat. It is as if we wanted to know Socrates and were told that Socrates is a man (in this instance, that the proletariat is not a man). In *Capital* we come somewhat closer to the idea of a class.

* Other thinkers conceive the modern individual's non-self as the void or nothingness. For Marx the "other" has a physiognomy more clearly defined than the self, since it is made up of social action through which alone in Marx's view the self achieves concreteness. It would seem to follow that the unhappy consciousness of our time is owing not so much to our being haunted by emptiness as by the presence of a social alter ego which we can neither become nor refuse to become.

The principle agents of this [capitalist] mode of production, the capitalist and the wage worker, are to that extent merely personifications of capital and wage labor. They are definite social characters assigned to individuals by the process of social production. They are the products of these definite social conditions of production.

Here the specific "materialistic connections" of capitalism are said to have produced two "definite social characters," the capitalist and the wage worker. Having been imposed upon individuals by modern production and thus made them identical with one another, these characters seem prepared to play the leading parts in the history of our epoch.

Upon closer examination, however, we note that the capitalist and the worker are here described as "mere personifications"; that is to say, they are metaphors of political economy rather than historical actors. They represent what Marx calls in the same passage the "peculiar traits" of capitalist production. They are like the little figures that illustrate statistical charts. In terms of theater, they belong among the *types* of melodrama or the morality play. Like First Murderer or Sir Avarice, they are reflections of a mode of behavior or a status. Collective persons of this species could only go on investing capital and working for wages.

In the Preface to *Capital*, Marx makes it clear that his "personifications" lack the power of choice and responsibility:

I paint the capitalist and the landlord in no sense *couleur de rose*. But here individuals are dealt with only in so far as they are personifications of economic categories, embodiments of particular class-relations and class-interests. My standpoint can . . . less than any other make the individual responsible for relations whose creature he socially remains, however much he may subjectively raise himself above them.

In *The German Ideology*, the class as personification has subsumed its members under an abstraction, which is part of a system of abstract relations. Individuals are absolved of responsibility for the actions of the class, and the class lacks human motivation, individual or collective. If the class struggles with other classes, it is not in order to affirm a common self or desire but because it is moved by the "contradictions" of the system of which it is an "agent."

Were history the struggle of such characters, how could Marx maintain, as he does, that "men make their own history"? A history made by personifications would be history made not by human beings, even human beings stirred by their own unreality, as under the rule of angels or heroes, but by embodied categories or elements of a process. Devoid of pathos, the conflict of these categories could hardly deserve Marx's description of a revolution as "the great historical tragedy." Philosophy would have been realized all too soon.

Nor, if the class man is a personification, does it have meaning to speak of a class as "revolutionary." The personification represents or incarnates—how can it overthrow that of which it is the sign? To personify labor, the worker need only work for wages; that of itself makes him a proletarian, nothing more is required. The "social character assigned" to him by his economic role does not forbid him to act politically as a reactionary or to think like a Buddhist. A class defined by statistics of production and consumption might be sufficient for economists of other schools concerned with behavior affecting markets. But it is the peculiarity of Marx's "political economy" that its author sees both the bourgeoisie and the proletariat in terms of revolution, and that he believes the class of workingmen to be destined to alter completely the conditions that created it. Such an active role cannot be attributed to a character that is but an embodiment of existing relations. For revolution an actor different from a personification is required.

In remarking that the worker or capitalist is a personification "only to that extent"—that is, in his economic role—Marx intimates that there are other dimensions to the class character. In his historical and polemical writings he speaks of the classes as full-bodied persons with egos that strive, dream, become conscious of themselves. The bourgeoisie in the opening pages of *The Eighteenth Brumaire* is a hero disguised as a Roman; the proletariat of *The Class Struggles in France* is "scarred, irreconcilable, unconquerable." There, beyond personifying an economic function, the class expresses its collective personality and acts with an intelligence and spirit peculiar to itself. That the essence of the class definition consisted for Marx in this active character-shaping spirit is implicit in his statement: "The working class is either revolutionary or it is nothing." Without being revolutionary the class would still represent the "materialistic connections" among workers, yet lacking the impulse of the historical mass actor the economic identity is nothing.

Are such references to the subjective state of a class mere examples of political rhetoric, like the femininity of France or the perfidiousness of Albion? Or are characterizations of its style and inner life to be taken as belonging to the full definition of a class? Unless we know if a certain kind of consciousness is indispensable to the historical existence of a class, the concept of the proletariat as an historical protagonist is not clear. In our day this question has taken on immense practical importance. If the working class is but an embodied economic category, it has no necessary part to play in the present historical situation, nor in the socialism that is presumed to be the next form of social organization—like the rest of mankind the workers will follow the guidance of politicians and ideologists, reformist, reactionary or revolutionary. If, however, the very existence of the proletariat presupposes the development in it of a socialist consciousness and will, its direct decisions and acts must be the basis of any change to be considered socialist—action by others in its name would be like action in behalf of any other idea. Thus the meaning of Marx's theory and its application to contemporary history turn on his conception of that mysterious social and metaphysical entity, which is at once an Idea that is a character and a community of struggling human beings that has the form of an Idea. If there is to be socialism, who will create it? And *what* is that *who?*

Marx's definition of the class as a personification appears near the end of Volume III of *Capital.* With some eagerness we pass to the next chapter. Having devoted his immense study to the impersonal processes by which modern man lives and falsifies himself, Marx now proposes to analyze "the great classes of modern society resting upon the capitalist mode of production." Says he: "The first question to be answered is this: What constitutes a class?" He is about to isolate the human substance in which the economic and historical become one, to exhibit the social organisms that we inhabit, that make us what we are, and by which we shall be carried into the future. We turn the page quickly—and are met by that classic declaration of mystery stories: HERE THE MANUSCRIPT ENDS.

I I

"All that is solid melts in the air, all that is holy is profaned . . ."

The Communist Manifesto

Capital breaks off without having described the transformation of the wretched personification of wage labor, that flesh-and-blood machine part fitted into modern production, into the future hero of history.* We are left with the dialectics of the earlier writings and with Marx's historical, agitational and programmatic works.

Dialectically, the mechanically impelled personification *must* turn into the conscious hero, since physical existence is, as it were, the evolutionary ground of human thinking and action. The material status of the working class will transform itself spontaneously into "self-activity," and its inevitable awakening will provide both the means of socialism and its aim. Thus, the working class is revolutionary by definition: it is formed "over against" another class; "with its birth," declares *The Communist Manifesto*, "begins its struggle with the bourgeoisie." The Buddhism of an individual workingman may therefore be disregarded; for his class becomes revolutionary through its material development and without regard to the thoughts of its members; when the time is ripe, this revolutionary class will "subsume" him, Buddhism and all, under its larger fate.

Accepting revolutionary consciousness as immanent in the proletariat, Marx's dialectics overleaps the problem of the emergence of proletarian radicalism as an historical fact. This is confirmed by Engels in a letter to Mehring eleven years after Marx's death:

We all laid, and were bound to lay, the main emphasis on the derivation of political, juridical and other ideological notions, and of the actions arising through the medium of these notions, from basic economic facts. But in so doing we neglected the formal side—the way in which these notions come about—for the sake of the content.

If not in Marx's analysis of capitalism, nor in his "dialectical materialist" method, where shall we discover Marx's

* The projected fourth volume of *Capital,* which Marx described to Engels as "the historical-literary one," was to have undertaken to do this.

conception of the classes as makers of history? Would it not be in those writings where he deals with the behavior of classes in actual revolutionary situations? There, it is no longer enough to characterize the classes in terms of the general development of society. And indeed, when he writes of the revolutions of his day, Marx does not "neglect the way in which their notions and actions came about," but examines the images and ideas that dominate the contending forces and result in what they do. Attempting to penetrate the motives of masses and their leaders in action, his method combines with his intuition to introduce a vocabulary of dramatic concepts including shaded Hegelianisms, peculiar to his thinking but often thoroughly "un-Marxian." These form a consistent outlook through the coherence of his metaphors and the recurrence of certain dramatic formulas—such as the resurrection of the dead in crises (theme of *The Eighteenth Brumaire*), the integrating effects of defeat (theme of *The Class Struggles in France*), the spontaneous correctness of the revolutionary act (*The Civil War in France*), the relevation through conflict of historical "secrets" (several works). Here, too, are signs of a "method"—or, if one prefers, of a unique cast of the imagination. What its connection is with Marxian materialism I shall not attempt to say. Suffice it that when so-called Marxist writings lack the inspiration of Marx's "rhetoric," distortion of the historical insight of the master is inevitable.

The self-consciousness that converts the class from an economic personification into an historical actor is not an intellectual comprehension of class interests and relations but is an aspect of the revolutionary act itself. Both class awareness and class identity arise out of class action. The class engages itself in the drama of history by its passionate and willful response to the poetry of the event. The style of its action constitutes the portrait of the class as an historical actor. Marx's image of the proletarian hero of history becomes visible in his characterization of the poetry of working-class upheaval. As befits the actor who is to terminate the historical drama, this poetry has a different relation to history than that of all previous collective actors:

The social revolution cannot draw its poetry from the past but only from the future. It cannot begin with itself before it has stripped off all superstitions in regard to the past. Earlier revolutions required world-historical recollections in order to drug themselves concerning their own content; the revolution of the nineteenth century must let the dead bury the dead. There the phrase went beyond the content; here the content goes beyond the phrase.
—*The Eighteenth Brumaire*

The proletarian revolution is to be characterized by its total abandonment of the past. It is to owe nothing to that repertory of heroic forms out of which history had supplied earlier revolutionists with the subjective means for meeting their situation. Other historical mass actors—nations, cults, bands, classes (including the "unheroic" bourgeoisie) —had, when bent on remaking the world, presented themselves on the stage in ancestral costume and with superhuman allies. The proletariat alone is to perform its part in everyday clothes and without sacrament. It is not to make itself capable of revolution by displacing itself with sublime models. Its revolution is to begin within itself as it is, not with a myth but with a "stripping off" of myths; the working class is to become in its mind and in its imagination exactly what it in fact is, the personification of wage labor. For the first time, human beings living under more or less identical conditions are to coalesce into a conscious active community without the aid of god or hero, prophet or leader, without rite of initiation or founding miracle, without visions, without ideals, without "the phrase that goes beyond the content."

The pastlessness of the proletarian revolution is thus the key to the character of the working class and its role. In a toast "to the proletarians of Europe," Marx declared:

For our part we do not mistake the shape of the shrewd spirit that continues to mark all these contradictions [between the productive forces and the social relations of our epoch]. We know that if the new-fangled forces of society are to work satisfactorily they need only be mastered by new-fangled men—and such are the workingmen. They are as much the invention of modern time as machinery itself. In the signs that bewilder the middle class, the aristocracy, and the poor prophets of regression, we recognize our old friend Robin Goodfellow, the old mole that can work in the earth so fast, that worthy pioneer —the revolution.

The proletarians are new men, an "invention of modern time." The spirit that agitates them is not Hamlet's "old mole" and "worthy pioneer," his father's ghost. The new hero never had a father; he sprang from the same source as the factory—the technological age. The shrewd spirit that informs him of his situation and prompts him to his act is no corpse risen from the grave. He lets the dead bury the dead. The spirit that speaks to him is the spirit of the future. The revolution *will* father the working class by giving birth to it as a human community. Without this inner spirit of revolt the workers are machines and lack historical existence; by revolution they achieve an identity and are converted into men.

An utterly new "invention," the proletariat is alien to the ancestral spirit. But in this alienation its inner condition faithfully reflects the epoch. For the mark of our era is that in it the past has lost its power to decide who a man is or to move him into action.

Constant revolutionizing of production, uninterrupted disturbance of all social conditions, everlasting uncertainty and agitation, distinguish the bourgeois epoch from all earlier ones. All fixed, fast-frozen relations, with their train of ancient and venerable prejudices and opinions, are swept away, all new formed ones become antiquated before they can ossify. All that is solid melts in the air, all that is holy is profaned, and man is at last compelled to face with sober senses his real conditions of life and his relations with his kind.

—*The Communist Manifesto*

The middle class has inaugurated the Modern. Its sign is the release of time and change into all human situations. What is not altered is swept away. No longer does history resemble a succession of friezes, with the old standing intact behind the new. The whole historical substance is in motion. No *deus ex machina* remains to step forward in historical crises to rescue the frustrated mass hero by converting businessmen into Romans, as in the French Revolution; farmers into Old Testament prophets, as in the British and American upheavals. No more Caesars, no more John Browns. Revolution through repetition of the past becomes impossible.*

Were proletarians "engaged in revolutionizing themselves and things . . . anxiously to conjure up the spirits of the past," as did their predecessors the bourgeoisie, their conjuring would remain unanswered. The "profaned past"

* Marx, and of course Marxists since Marx, obviously underestimated the power of the past to initiate historical actions; our century is a jungle of revivals. But Marx seems correct as to the exhaustion of the *creative* power of the past, in that the revival of old forms (e.g., Kennedy's "New Frontier," De Gaulle's "Crusade") no longer appears capable of moving society forward through "creating something entirely new."

will not communicate with these children of the machine, nor will it provide them with heroic masks. One spirit alone can move the workers, the shrewd spirit that challenges "the real conditions."

In that its own pastlessness corresponds most completely to that of the modern world, the proletariat stands as the protagonist of present-day mankind. To it Marx put the question of creative action deprived of the guidance of tradition. The liquefaction of the past gives the word "pioneer" a literal application to the cultural condition of the workingman. Like men isolated in a desert of space, this class laboring in the very core of industrial society is to derive a collective originality from the emptiness of its time relation. The mind of Marx's working class exists in the *as if* of an American or African wilderness. For it, as for the avant-garde poet, Europe is strewn with "poetic old junk"; no more than the self-estranged artist can this mass, produced entirely by the economic needs of society and stranger to its inherited forms, hope to achieve its human "other self" through appropriating an existing poetry. Rimbaud's banner: "It is necessary to be absolutely modern," is raised over the revolution of new-fangled men which is to take place without recourse to the higher powers of the dead. With everything solid melted into the air, only what they themselves create can have reality for them. The everlasting uncertainty of capitalist society has with them given rise to human beings whose normal life is uncertainty, and who therefore can satisfy themselves only through endlessly changing their own nature as they endlessly remake the conditions of their lives through "the revolution in permanence."

"I enter the true kingdom of the sons of Ham," announced Rimbaud. For his part Marx does not hesitate to designate as "barbarian" his hero of the modern for whom the past has no gifts. The proletariat is a barbarian in exactly the same sense that the American is, traditionally, Europe's barbarian. Estranged from the accumulations of culture in the Old World, both appear as tossing in Rimbaud's "drunken boat" toward who knows what "incredible Floridas" of the future. Like an American and the things he surrounds himself with, the proletarian and the "commodity" he produces lack that saturation with the centuries that for Europe is synonymous with cultural value and spiritual presence. "To our grandparents," said Rilke,

a "house," a "well," a tower familiar to them, even their own dress, their cloak, was still infinitely more, infinitely more intimate; almost each thing, a vessel in which they found something human and into which they set aside something human. Now, from America, empty indifferent things are crowding over to us, sham things, *life decoys.* . . . A house, in the American understanding, an American apple or a grapevine there, has nothing in common with the house, the fruit, the grape, into which went the hopes and meditations of our forefathers. . . . We are perhaps the last still to have known such things.

The proletariat is of this "American" sphere, in which persons, places, things, human relations, exist without the time dimension.* "To detach a fact from its origin," said

* Naturally, Americans resent being called "barbarians" by European aristocrats, pseudo-aristocrats and their native imitators, whose attacks on America are inseparable from their contempt for "modern mass man," of whom America is supposed to be the typical product. One effect of American indignation is to play down the difference in spiritual form of a nation with a past of immigration, pioneering and democratic revolts. The official American view is that America has culture, too; in other words, an inheritance like any other country. Yet American writers and artists know through experience that they cannot hope to define themselves as individuals so long as they follow European models in respect to the past, even a past of their own. *"Moi, je suis barbare,"* defiantly declared a character in one of Dostoyevsky's stories. It would be a gain for American consciousness if it, too, boldly accepted its predicament as a nation (aging) of "new men."

the French philosopher Lévinas recently, "is precisely to live in the modern world."

For Rilke the world had been made human by familiarity and meditation. The American does not meditate, he acts. So, too, in Marx's view, does the proletariat, whose self-consciousness arises through the "practical movement." Both these heirs of the capitalist principle of uninterrupted activity seem cast for the same role: to be the agent of history in annihilating all cultural survivals. The dissolution by capitalism of fixed sacred and human relations has been carried to an extreme degree by the Americans and awaits completion by "the proletarian hordes."*

If stability, authority, sacrament are needed to make men human, what but civilization's doom is the American-proletarian world? The old subjectivity, born of slow crystallizations of feeling, finds it necessary to fight for its life against the spirit of action and change that rules the newfangled men. Insensible to dramatic issues in a state of development, liberalism obscures this fatal struggle by its pragmatic compromises. In contrast, Marx places his bet for the future on the proletarian revolution which "cannot draw its poetry from the past," and, brushing aside the liberal veil, squarely proclaims himself the foe of the pastist spirituality of Europe. Democracy, the proletariat, will triumph, yet civilization will not perish. In a world denuded of symbolic value by ceaseless activity, a new humanism has become possible, that of men soberly responding to their real conditions and relations. In place of sacred sentiments found or secreted in things, a secular spirituality will re-

* Flaubert's plan for the conclusion of *Bouvard et Pécuchet* presents the typical cultured European's prophecy of American-proletarian doom. "Pécuchet sees the future of humanity in dark colors. The modern man is lessened, and has become a machine. . . . There will be no longer ideal, religion, morality. The United States will have conquered the earth. Universal greed. There will be no longer anything but a debauch of workmen."

create itself from moment to moment out of free, conscious action in living situations. Its poetry will spring not from the stillness of the past but from movement toward the future, not from time come to rest but from time as change, not from the dead but from what is being born, not from the human as heritage but from the needs of humanity.

Many of the attributes of the proletariat as the potential embodiment of the spirit of the modern are, inescapably, attributes of the American,* unquestionably the best available model of the new-fangled; from Marx to Lenin to Trotsky, American practices have been cited to illustrate qualities needed under socialism. Free of traditional restraints, the American stakes everything on acting in his own interests. Nothing "in" objects or men checks him from changing or replacing them. Transforming landscapes, materials, memories, he "takes things in his stride," "finds the right man for the right job." He converts the past itself into a tool;† to a significant degree he has realized Marx's vision of communism as a society in which "the present dominates the past."

But though the American is a natural representative of the modern, his situation does not impel him to make himself its hero. The pioneering out of which he arose is not

---

* In comparing the American and the proletariat we are thinking of them, of course, not as categories, where they overlap (since many Americans are wage workers), but as collective entities or types—the first actual, the second hypothetical.

† "The Americans," complained Goebbels with comic envy, "have the ability of taking their relatively small stock of culture and by a modernized version to make of it something that is very à propos for the present time. We are loaded down altogether too much with tradition and piety. We hesitate to clothe our cultural heritage in modern dress. It therefore remains purely historical or museum-like. . . . The cultural heritage of our past can be rendered fruitful for the present on a large scale only if we present it with modern means. The Americans are masters at this sort of thing, I suppose because they are not weighed down as much as we with historical ballast. Nevertheless we shall have to do something about it"— *The Goebbels Diaries.*

forced upon him as a continuing necessity. His material accomplishments provide him with room in which to rest; his history has been one of setting limits to his revolutionizing. For all the audacity of his behavior the American does not place himself in principled opposition to the past, nor challenge tradition as the champion of a new conception of spirit based on ceaseless activity.* He refuses to will, and make himself responsible for, his destruction of the time sanctified. The American acts in silence, so to speak, permitting his consciousness and his conscience to remain bound by values inherited from Europe. In America, Marx pointed out, "the feverishly youthful movement of material production, that has a new world to make its own, has left neither time nor opportunity for abolishing the old spirit world." Like nature, America accepts with equanimity whatever (be it slaveholding or travel by donkey) succeeds in surviving the processes of American development. The American's essential outlook is that of the tourist; for him the world is a picturesque surface, and whatever needs to be changed will be taken care of when he gets back to work.

The proletariat, however, is not permitted by its position to give a limited expression to its modernity. Severed from the past, devoid of the various cultural forms through which other groups (e.g., nationalists, church members, art lovers) attempt to define themselves as human beings within the universal "agitation," the workingman can conceive himself as both a workingman and a human being only in undertaking projects. To him action is the essence of being a man. Yet he is not permitted to act, for his movements are controlled by others. His labor is central to

* America was closer to delivering such a challenge a century ago (as expressed in Whitman's "Prefaces," for example) than it is at present, when its past-destroying action having expanded to world dimensions, it hesitates to attack *any* tradition.

the transforming process of modern industry, yet he neither decides what is to be transformed nor does he imprint his likeness on the finished thing. As a "pioneer" in creating the new technological world, he could be a man; actually, he is bound to the machine and can initiate nothing and make nothing his. In this exclusion from the beginning and end of his action, Marx concluded, the proletariat must recognize itself as a tool deprived of humanity.

As the American is the free man and master of the industrial epoch, even when he ignores the implications of his freedom and his mastery, the proletarian is its inherent victim. He represents the internal flaw of the modern, its original sin. While everything about him is revolutionized, he alone is held in a fixed relation. The ceaseless upsetting of ancestral orders has other victims—the proletariat stands apart from them all. Throughout the globe, aristocrats, priestly castes, ancient races clinging to their traditions or prevented from abandoning them, are plunged into crisis by "profaning" capitalism. Yet as individuals any of these can, like Ruggles of Red Gap or a Reform rabbi, find his place in the modern world if—and this is the struggle of liberalism—the "time stigma" of his group is dissolved, so that he can bring himself up to date and start afresh as a citizen. The misery of the workingman alone cannot be ameliorated through synchronizing him with his epoch. He suffers *in* and through his presentness, as one totally immersed in contemporary life. Stemming entirely from his part in it, his discontent is central to the movement of modern history. *The proletariat is the modern itself experienced as misery.*

For the American action is a natural response to need or desire (whether his action can satisfy that need is another question). For the worker action is but a possibility, the anguishing possibility of transforming himself into an individual. Hemmed in on the bare, functional stage of industrial production, altogether *there,* without past or vision of paradise, he is, except for this possibility of acting, a mere prop, a thing that personifies. Speaking half figuratively,* to become a human being the proletarian must "Americanize" himself, that is, overcome the void of his past by making a new self through his actions.

Yet all the relations of capitalist society forbid the working class to act except as a tool. Hence its free act must be a revolutionary act, one that must subdue "all existing conditions" and can set itself no limits. The proletarian victim of the modern cannot enter the historical drama as an actor without becoming its hero. In "the indefinite prodigiousness of their aims," as Marx described them in *The Eighteenth Brumaire,* the workers signify that with them revolution is a need of the spirit, a means of redemption. Before Marx's internal pioneer opens a frontier without end.

---

* Only *half* figuratively, since becoming Americans has been the actual salvation chosen by millions of workingmen from older nations. With the proletariat there is more to the impulse to become an American than the desire for economic opportunity, flight from oppression, etc. Primarily, it is a will to enter a world where the past no longer dominates, and where therefore that creature of the present, the workingman, can merge himself into the human whole. Thus proletarians immigrate to America in a different spirit from middle-class people or peasants, who from the moment they enter "American time" experience it as something disconcerting and even immoral, and whose nostalgia for their homelands and customs is often communicated from one generation to the next. But America's thin time crust, that seems so desolate to immigrants of other classes, is precisely what satisfies the proletariat and has provided so many workers with the energy to become leaders of industry. Becoming an American is a kind of revolution for foreign proletarians, though it is a magical revolution rather than a revolutionary act. It alters the workingman's consciousness of himself; like a religious conversion it supplies him with a new identity. But this change does not extinguish his previous situation as a character in the capitalist drama; he is still in the realm of economic personifications. As an American, too, a social-economic role will be assigned to him: worker, farmer, capitalist. The elimination of these abstract types continues to call for a transformation of the historical "plot."

"Communism . . . turns existing conditions into conditions of unity."

— *The German Ideology*

The figure of the permanent pioneer is implied by the presence in society of men united by actions which respond to actual conditions (i.e., those of factory production), without reference to the past. All the high hopes and promises of socialism rest upon this human force supposedly representing our mythless situation. The community to be founded by the featureless metaphors of wage labor, to whom everything human is but a possibility which they must bring to life for themselves, would be like no other community in history. Its existence would of itself destroy the root of all spiritual miseries—the hallucinatory nature of social life.

The illusory community, in which individuals have up till now combined, always took on an independent existence in relation to them, and was at the same time, since it was the combination of one class over against another, not only a completely illusory community, but a new fetter as well. In the real community the individuals obtain their freedom in and through their association.

—*The German Ideology*

The community as the supremely fantastic "being" that regulates our behavior renders us incommensurate with reality and generates those false selves which have always turned human lives into comedies and tragedies of mistaken identity.* In contrast, a community that is nothing else than the united action of its members in their common situation must cause the phantoms that beset us to disappear.

"The reality which communism creates," *The German Ideology* explains, "is precisely the real basis for rendering it impossible that anything should exist independently of individuals." No institutions, idols, programs, none of Blake's hated "Mental Deities" standing above the human being and acting as his master. No longer is each individual haunted by an alien "I" detached from his daily life and hovering over it with threats or promises of salvation. The stage of history ceases to be invaded by the banners and uniforms of unpredictable mass egos called into being by prophets or heroes. In place of warring cults, states, classes, each individual meditates his next creation. Man, released from his sad history as Frenchman or Russian, Jew or Hindu, has ceased to be an abstraction and a prey to abstractions.

Through having been submitted by capitalism to uniform conditions, and through having turned those conditions into "conditions of unity," socialist society recaptures the organic coherence lacking in collective life since primitive times. Yet this unseparated state is experienced by the individual as absolute freedom. No longer an entity independent of its individual members and opposed to their desires, the community has become the individuals

---

* Like Kierkegaard, Marx recognized that man takes up the slack between himself and social reality by creating illusory selves. To this fate Kierkegaard responded with the Christian-Romantic program of "becoming infinitely subjective"—the individual resigns himself to the incommensurability and puts reality behind him through withdrawing from the social and historical in the direction of the self in its "god-relation." The classicist Marx sees an opposite movement, the outward one that harmonizes man and the world through changing the world into something altogether human.

themselves in their real interrelationship. Each is equivalent to the whole; for each is joined to the whole not through surrender to its symbols but by concrete extension of his own being. A spontaneous passionate communion, as in invasions, floods, celebrations, becomes the normal state. With solidarity ensured by genuine self-interest, the drama of choice between revolt and submission becomes an anachronism, and with it the poetries of worship and blasphemy. In the language of *Capital,* the life process of society strips off its mystical veil.

Neither pastist nor futurist, altogether immersed in the living moment, man has at last gained a capacity for change —with a kind of Renaissance zest, yet unmotivated to violence, he revels in action as his proper medium. "A touch of your finger on the drum," said Rimbaud, "sets loose all the sounds and begins the new harmony." The individual conceives his existence in terms of creations which in totally satisfying him are serviceable to mankind. Connoisseur of time, he gives himself entirely to these adventures of his whole being with an inwardness that draws from the consciousness of death the savor of each instant. His daily life is an enactment of Hegelian dialectic as summarized by Marx:

it includes in its comprehension an affirmative recognition of the existing state of things, at the same time also, the recognition of the negation of that state, of its inevitable breaking up.
—*Capital*

A universal secular and productive community is a rational projection of the material and cultural conditions introduced by the technological revolution. Marx saw, however, that the achievement of a free, classless society required more than a program which humanity could be urged to carry out. It needed a specific human agency in which a passion for freedom and equality was implicit. The *what* needed a *who*. Socialism, like any other new form, demanded its creator—at a basic level, its proposition is an aesthetic one. We have seen that with Marx proletarian revolution called for the inner alteration of men on a mass scale. For a transformation of this magnitude to take place under the inspiration of "the real conditions," and without the stimulant of myth, a new principle of self-creation had to become effective. The birth of the reality-inspired "I" of the proletariat in workingmen throughout the world is the initiating act of Marx's drama of the overthrow of capital-ism—and in the rise and fall of this mass self-transforma-tion lies the pathos of the socialist movement.

The anguish of the working class arises, with tragic irony, from the same source as its potential grandeur: that this class has no positive (as distinguished from statistical) existence, except through the collective action of its mem-bers; its style in food, dress or manners, for example, merges wherever possible into that of strata above it. Nor is the proletariat a brotherhood which the individual work-ingman can join, like a nation or a church. He can affiliate himself with creations of the organized labor movement—a union or labor party, for example—but these have the character given to them by their leaders, not by the class as such. Only when the workingman participates in a particu-lar struggle is he humanly identified as a proletarian. As it lacks anchorage in the past, his class lacks it also in the ideal.

Communism is for us not a stable state which is to be estab-lished, an ideal to which reality will have to adjust itself. We call communism the *real* movement which abolishes the present state of things. The conditions of this movement result from the premises now in existence.

—*The German Ideology*

The proletariat must create itself and continue to create itself in revolutionary action; at rest it has no identity.

The unhinging of the consciousness of the proletariat from the past as well as from an imagined future causes its action to take on, Marx repeatedly reminds us, a unique historical form. All earlier revolutions derived their power of action from fantasy; that of the workers is to be tied to the facts and is to be soberly realistic. A new tragic dynamics is to be at work. The creation of an identity out of nothing, instead of the recognition of an existing, if hidden, "I." With the middle class, Marx explains, self-recognition takes place in an ecstatic leap which overwhelms all distinctions of time and circumstance. Having discovered their model in antiquity, "bourgeois revolutions storm ever more swiftly from success to success; their dramatic effects outdo each other; men and things seem set in sparkling brilliants; ecstasy is the everyday spirit" (*The Eighteenth Brumaire*). Romanticism led the middle class to victory, but the self-affirmation of the working class is immeasurably more arduous:

Proletarian revolutions, on the other hand, criticize themselves constantly, interrupt themselves continually in their own course, come back to the apparently accomplished in order to recommence it afresh, deride with unmerciful thoroughness the inadequacies, weaknesses and paltrinesses of their first attempts, seem to throw down their adversary only in order that he may draw new strength from the earth and rise again more gigantic before them, recoil ever and anon from the indefinite prodigiousness of their own aims, until the situation has been created which makes all turning back impossible and the conditions themselves cry out: *Hic Rhodus, hic salta! Hier ist die Rose, hier tanze!*

Its distance from the poetry of the past deprives the proletariat of the ability to lose itself in grand gestures. Can its sobriety, however, supply it with inner continuity? So long as its situation fluctuates, its action must fluctuate with it. But since its action alone causes it to be, its existence is an oscillation between struggle and nothingness. Thus constant self-scrutiny marks its revolutionary style— Baudelarian in contrast to the Hugoesque enthusiasm of the bourgeoisie; for without persistent criticism how can it be sure that its action is in its own interest and not in the service of others? At all points, working-class actions betray a sense of inner incompletion, of the doubt of the class with respect to its identity and its motives. With its "indefinitely prodigious aims," it starts again and again from the beginning, as if confessing its own nullity between one effort and the next.

Controlled by historical change, the proletariat can be rescued from periodicity only through being subjected by external conditions to a steady pressure within a constantly narrowing area of choice, "until the situation has been created that makes all turning back impossible." The primary condition, therefore, for the conversion of the proletariat from a personification into an actor is the "growing mass of misery" predicted by Marx. A steadily worsening crisis is needed to keep the working class present upon the stage of history and to bring coherence and direction to its movements.

Yet even if the situation of the workers were to reach the vanishing point of human endurance (by what measure?), the socialist revolution could not begin unless the proletariat, preserving the immediacy of its response to conditions, and resisting in impermeable sobriety the rise of new myths, could recognize that the occasion had come for its final assault. According to Marx, however, it is precisely those conditions that make living in the actual world intolerable that cause people to remove themselves to worlds of the imagination. By this rule, the growing misery of the proletariat must tend to force it into increasing fantasy. But when the workers, intoxicated with fictions and ideologies, surrender themselves to "alien bonds," the class breaks up and abandons its role. Hardship can be the basis of unity only if the minds of the workers remain purged of dreams or ideas that might soften their situation or carry them beyond it. To achieve immediate and accurate response to events as its habitual mode of historical consciousness, the proletariat must have "nothing to lose but its chains," in the intellectual and emotional as well as in the economic and social sense. Along with the "asceticizing" of their physical existence by the hostile process in which they are trapped, a disciplined asceticism of the imagination must hold them to the severity of their economic category. The growing mass of misery must be matched by a growing mass of emptiness. In order that the mask may become human, the man must have willed to become nothing but the mask.

Hence, as Lenin insisted, though with a conclusion which we shall examine later, *the most extreme conditions cannot guarantee the revolutionary unification of the workers.* Their unity must begin in an inner undertaking: that of willing to make themselves the suffering abstraction which their role in production implies that they are.

Before the proletariat lies the pathetic choice: either to remain through inactivity *historically* nothing as a class, or to become *humanly* nothing in order to rid itself of any considerations other than the demands of its historical situation. As individuals, either to accept their inability to act for themselves so long as they remain wage workers, or to form a collectivity of their own through throwing themselves into the limitless adventure of the revolution in permanence. As a revolutionist, the proletarian must be prepared to die in order to exist, and for nothing else.

"They have no ideals to realize but to set free the elements of the new society with which old collapsing bourgeois society is itself pregnant. . . . The great social measure of the Commune was its own working existence" (*The Civil War in France*). Only if the proletariat can sustain in itself the tragic dialectics of history and be ready to sacrifice itself for whatever the moment asks of it can it "realize philosophy." Gratuitousness is the sovereign requirement of genuinely secular (without ideologies, without myths) historical creation. Act in order to avoid being acted upon.

I V

"When shall we . . . salute the birth of the new labor, the new wisdom, the flight of tyrants and demons?"

RIMBAUD

The mythless proletariat suffering with naked consciousness the trials of its position is a tragic concept on a heroic scale. One understands why Marx criticized Lassalle's historical tragedy, *Franz von Sickingen,* for making "political unity its chief idea." "You should have *Shakespearized* more," Marx wrote. "As it is, I consider your greatest fault to be *Schillerization,* the transformation of individuals into mere mouthpieces of the spirit of the age." Against the romantic bourgeois revolution, with its rhetoric, its gestures, its costumes, he had placed a figure that had yet to define itself. As with Aristotle, the plot of the Marxian drama of history "comes before" the hero. A sober Sophoclean victim of given facts, he is pushed toward his doom by contradictions from which nothing can save him, for the concrete means for their solution do not yet exist.* The struggles induced by his misery are not, however, in vain. Constituting his existence, they bring about a clarification of his consciousness and a ripening of his ability to act. In the descending scale of his fortunes his illusions fall away one by one until his identity reveals itself, not in words but in unavoidable acts, and the tragedy is resolved in a transcendence.

To the extent that its plot conforms to modern political conflicts, Marx's grand drama is a profound hypothesis regarding society's future. It cannot, however, be more than an hypothesis, since its outcome depends upon the subjective capacity of actual workingmen to perform the role of the proletarian hero, and this in turn depends upon the clarity of their consciousness and their ability to act together. Marx, however, refused to regard proletarian action as an *if* of creative inspiration. For him the revolution was a certainty guaranteed by science. Analysis of capitalist accumulation revealed the inevitable build-up of pressure on the proletariat that was bound to shape the class into the agent of history.

From this translation of the dramatic into the "scientific" arise the basic ambiguities of Marxist politics. Accepting the revolutionary proletariat as an hypothesis, the socialist would look for the emergence of the heroic image in the actual struggles of the working class and in the rhetoric of its action. In each effort of the class, laden with suspense and pathos, he would measure the degree to which

* "Historical action is to yield to their personal inventive action," Marx wrote contemptuously of the Utopians; "historically created conditions of emancipation to fantastic ones; and the gradual, spontaneous class organization of the proletariat to an organization of society specially contrived by these inventors. Future history resolves itself in their eyes into the propaganda and practical carrying out of their social plans"—*The Communist Manifesto.*

the values attached by Marx to the proletarian image were in the way of being realized. With Marx, however, all particular efforts of living workers are subsumed under the *concept* of the class-conscious proletariat and regarded as incomplete manifestations of the final conflict. Though he thinks of the revolution as a tragedy, Marx does not experience its incidents as tragic but rather as "lessons" (one of the most popular words in the Marxian lexicon), and his work lacks the pathetic tonality appropriate to its notion of the workers transforming themselves through constant risk of their lives. The rationalism of Marx's prose favorites, Diderot, Voltaire, wins against his beloved Aeschylus and Shakespeare. An optimism with respect to the historical drama as a whole sweetens for the spectator the anguish of the hero's striving. Even in his description of the Paris Commune and its executioners, the peak of his revolutionary eloquence, it is the *foes* of the revolution that Marx most vividly evokes. Concerning the peculiar state of mind that must have prevailed among these "pioneers" of history, so strangely isolated in time and place; of their relations with one another; of their sense of what lay ahead, he takes little notice. To the pathos of this momentary foreshadowing of communism in flesh and blood, he responds only with moral passion and prophecy. For him the Commune is a single lost battle in a war that can have but one outcome, the triumph of socialism. Thus Marx himself prepares the shallow trust of Marxism in deterministic formulas.

In making socialism scientific, Marx attempts to guarantee the appearance of the proletariat as actor in two ways. The first is through metaphysics. In his Introduction to *The Living Thoughts of Karl Marx,* Trotsky summarizes this position: "The productive forces need a new organizer and a new master, and, *since existence determines con-*

sciousness, Marx had no doubt that the working class, at the cost of errors and defeats, will come to understand the actual situation, and, sooner or later, will draw the imperative practical conclusions" (my italics). But this statement fails to take into account the inescapability of illusion in epochs of crises indicated by Marx. Nor can the proposition that existence determines consciousness, assuming that it is correct, be relied on to produce the *particular* kind of consciousness (revolutionary) anticipated by Marx. If Marx could be aware in advance of the necessary effect of their situation on the minds of the workers, his consciousness would have preceded existence, which is in violation of the proposition. It might be answered that the capitalist situation already existed in Marx's time, and that it is the development of that situation, first understood by him, that the workers will come to grasp. But this would be to detach the economic situation from the human beings in it and to conceive it as unaffected by changes in their consciousness. Within the movement of capitalism Marx might predict the general direction of certain processes—concentration of capital, acceleration of crises, and so on—but he cannot predict the total situation of the workers, which includes the history of their response (or lack of it) to their situation. Yet nothing less than this total situation can be meant by "existence" in its determination of consciousness.

For Marx, capitalist production was a revolutionizing force; and since the workers sprang from this context they, too, would be revolutionary. But the revolutionizing processes of capitalism would of themselves only instill in the worker a negative attitude toward old ideas, beliefs, methods (which has, more or less, proved to be the case); it would not illuminate the worker about himself nor unite him actively with other workers. If the consciousness of the proletariat is a mere "reflection" of its existence under capitalism, it will tend toward apathy rather than revolution. If, on the other hand, the existence that determines proletarian consciousness comprises its changing mood, the class simply is what it is, and may or may not revolt.* Marxism must either reduce the historical situation to a number of external elements definable in advance, and thus become a mechanical system, or "vulgar materialism"; or it must admit that it can predict nothing concerning the consciousness of the proletariat and its action, in which case its drama of change remains an hypothesis and not a predictable certainty.

The failure of "existence" to give rise to revolutionary consciousness led Marx and Marxists to a second type of effort to guarantee the revolution: through politics and propaganda. In his letter to Mehring quoted above, Engels recognized the failure of the "basic economic facts" to account for "the way in which these notions [political, juridical, ideological] come about." That same year (1893) he indicates some of the consequences of that failure for Marxism. In the revolution of 1848, he recalls in his Introduction to *The Class Struggles in France,* Marx relied upon the masses' understanding of their historical situation to sustain the continuity of their revolutionary spirit:

The proletarian masses themselves, even in Paris, after the victory, were still absolutely in the dark as to the path to be taken. And yet the movement was there, instinctive, spontaneous, irrepressible. Was not this just the situation in which a revolution had to succeed? . . . If, in all the longer revolutionary periods,

* Trotsky seems to overlook the fact that for the workers "to understand the actual situation" means not only a consciousness of objective relations and the drawing of "practical conclusions" but an awareness of themselves and their strength, which can come about only in the course of the action. Had Trotsky considered the primacy of this subjective condition, stressed by Rosa Luxemburg, he would have found it even more difficult than he did to accept the Bolshevik theory of the Party and the masses.

it was so easy to win the great masses of the people by the merely plausible and delusive views of the minorities thrusting themselves forward, how could they be less susceptible to *ideas which were the truest reflex of their economic position, which were nothing but the clear, comprehensible expression of their needs, of needs not yet understood by themselves, but only vaguely felt.* To be sure, this revolutionary mood of the masses had almost always, and usually very speedily, given way to lassitude or even to a revulsion to its opposite, as soon as illusion evaporated and disappointment set in. But here it was not a question of delusive views . . . (my italics).

His social-economic analysis had convinced Marx that the proletariat was, objectively, powerful enough to overcome the government. Since existence determines consciousness, the workers had already "vaguely" grasped the truth of their position. All that was needed was to clarify this awareness with ideas which were nothing else than what they already knew. The "instinctive movement" would thereupon be sustained by consciousness against the usual collapse into disillusioned apathy; and "the proletariat grown wise by experience must become the decisive factor."

The "ideas which were the truest reflex" failed, however, to produce this steadying effect. "History," Engels goes on to say, "has proved us, and all who thought like us, wrong." Not wrong in relying on the truth, but wrong, he explains, in estimating the situation—it was not ripe for proletarian revolution. This mistake raises numerous questions, ignored by Engels, regarding the determination of consciousness. Does the diminishing of the fervor of the masses in 1848 signify that they were more conscious than Marx of their situation, instinctively aware of its unripeness? So it would seem, since their abandonment of revolution conformed to the real position, while Marx's notion of it did not. But if the masses acted correctly without the Marxian "reflex of their economic position," and even in opposition to it, what is the funciton of the reflex? Also, should it not be admitted that the mood of the masses, since their existence is most directly affected, is a better measure of the situation than the Marxian analysis? Another point: had Marx correctly estimated the "unripe" situation of 1848, his truth could not have had the effect of maintaining revolutionary fervor. We know that when he doubted the ripeness of the situation or the readiness of the proletariat Marx counciled wary support of middle-class progressive aims, while warning the workers against too-high hopes. He strove to check fervor by criticism rather than to heighten and maintain it. Would not such dispelling of illusion at the start of revolt have had the same effect as the bitter awakening described by Engels, that of depleting the masses' revolutionary energy? It depletes it sooner, so that in its effect "truth" is the same as reactionary propaganda.

At any rate, Engels's confession of error would have been more magnanimous if, giving full weight to the consequences of even once misleading the workers, he had inquired into the dangers of Marxian certainty and of its tendency to reverse its philosophy in practice by ascribing to its own program the finality of existence itself. Instead, Engels proceeds to argue that by 1893 history has corrected its earlier deficiencies and that the situation has now matured for proletarian revolution. Evidence of this is the acceptance by the workers of "the theory of Marx, sharply formulating the final aims of the struggle." Apparently, existence and consciousness have been firmly welded together at last:

At that time the masses, sundered and differing according to locality and nationality, linked only by the feeling of common suffering, undeveloped, tossed to and fro in their perplexity from enthusiasm to despair; today a great international army of Socialists, marching irresistibly on and daily growing in number, organization, discipline, insight and assurance of victory.

The collective "I" of the proletariat has finally defined itself—it has become the Party. Proletarian unity and action, conceived as an anguished response to the real conditions and "having no ideals to realize," has become a disciplined, self-assured "march" toward defined aims. Proletarian consciousness, once consisting of "the content and material of its revolutionary activity," has become Marxist theory.*

Engels seems unaware that what he is describing as an historical development is to an equal degree a decisive shift in Marxist philosophy, that its reliance upon existence to supply the proletariat with a self and an intelligence has been quietly abandoned in favor of Party ideology and discipline. His contention that the rise of a marching Party reflects the changed position of the proletariat cannot eliminate the qualitative difference between the kind of concrete intelligence that arises spontaneously in the course of a battle and the stratagems deduced by leaders from the place of the event in their scenario of history. If "existence determines consciousness" means the same thing in both instances, Dunkirk would be identical with the procedures of the British occupation army. A revolutionary consciousness that responds directly to what is *in* the situation, and corrects its theories by that response, must in regard to

---

* Contrast Engels's statement with the following text of Marx four decades earlier: "A class in which the revolutionary interests of society are concentrated, so soon as it has risen up, finds directly in its own situation the content and material of its revolutionary activity: foes to be laid low, measures dictated by the needs of the struggle to be taken; the consequences of its own deeds drive it on. It makes no theoretical inquiries into its own task."

every problem reach different practical conclusions from those of a Party consciousness guided by the theory of "the final aims of the struggle."

For Engels in 1893 the revolutionary struggle is no longer subject to the intermittences of the heart and mind of the working class; nor does its continuity depend upon the reflexes of a proletariat forced to revolt by its deepening misery. "In order that the masses may understand what is to be done, long, persistent work is required, and it is just this work which we are now pursuing, and with a success which drives the enemy to despair." Instead of learning in action, the working class has been put to school by the Party; it *marches* with its will in the secure custody of the Marxists. Marching has indeed replaced revolutionary action, the movement which was to have been the source itself of the "alteration" of the workers.* The "decisive shock force of the international proletarian army" has become, says Engels, the two million voters of the German Social Democracy and their allies. "We, the 'revolutionaries,' the 'rebels,' " he observes complacently, noting that "the irony of world history turns everything upside down" —"we are thriving far better on legal methods than on illegal methods and revolt." With the military language— "shock troops," "army"—and with "revolutionaries" in quotes, what has become of the shrewd spirit and the notion that the working class makes itself human only through revolt?

Was Engels's conversion of Marx's drama of history—assumed to be inherent in events—into a didactic fable of socialist politics a betrayal of the master's thought a decade after his death? In no respect. Marx, too, had attempted to

---

* "Both for the production on a mass scale of this communist consciousness, and for the success of the cause itself, the alteration of men on a mass scale is necessary; an alteration which can only take place in a practical movement, a revolution"—*The German Ideology.*

overcome by political means the laggardness of existence in producing revolutionary consciousness.

If this country [England] is the classic seat of landlordism and capitalism, by virtue of that fact it is also here that the material conditions of their destruction are most highly developed. The General Council [dominated by Marx] being at present placed in the happy position of having its hand directly on this great lever of the proletarian revolution . . . it would be sheer folly, we would almost say it would be an outright crime, to allow that hold to fall into purely English hands!

The English have all the material requisites necessary for the social revolution. What they lack is the spirit of generalization and revolutionary ardor. *It is only the General Council which can supply this deficiency,* which can thus accelerate the truly revolutionary movement in this country and consequently everywhere. . . . As the General Council we can initiate measures which later, in the public execution of their tasks, appear as spontaneous movements of the English working class—"Resolution of the General Council of the International Workingmen's Association," January 1, 1870 (my italics).

Somehow the material conditions have failed in England to transform themselves into ideas and ardor, and Marx holds it to be criminal folly to depend upon them to do so. He proposes to substitute himself for the mass "I" of the British proletariat in order to originate its acts. Yet he has no intention of formally rejecting his doctrine of immanence and self-emancipation. He wishes his acts to "appear as spontaneous movements of the English working class." And if accused of Machiavellianism, he has already replied that by supplying the absent ego of the class he is but "accelerating the truly revolutionary movement" called for by his historical script.

Marx's passage from philosophy to instigation seems a vacillation induced by the disappointing course of events rather than a conclusive change of outlook. Upheavals like the Commune or the American Civil War restore his perspective of spectator and prompter of the historical drama as it develops through the interplay of its class actors. The laws of history then appear to him to be asserting themselves ironically against *all* programs. Engels, too, confronted by revolutionary action, but without the "great lever" at hand to tempt him, rests his expectations on dramatic irony: in 1885 he writes to Zasulich concerning Russia, where no Marxist organization existed:

People who boasted that they had *made* a revolution have always seen the next day that they had no idea what they were doing, that the revolution they *made* did not in the least resemble the one they would have liked to make. That is what Hegel calls the irony of history, an irony that few historic personalities escape. [His italics.]

When the drama is being physically enacted, Hegel's dialectics reenters "materialism" and displaces doctrinaire politics.

What has evidently proved unendurable to philosophers of class conflict is the discontinuity of the drama, the long intermissions in which the proletarian protagonist vanishes from the stage of history. Theoretically, the revolution is always in progress, with an ever present proletariat growing more active and class conscious. In actuality, the action on the stage keeps breaking down as the "contradictory" process of development fails to translate itself into human conflict. Revolts are far apart, and when they do occur prove to be but moments of indefinite duration and effect. Even worse than the discontinuity of the action is the discontinuity of the collective hero. Social peace, disintegrating the working class into individuals with non-class identifications, causes the proletariat to fade back into an economic metaphor and to become an historical nothing.

The intellectual void in the working class as conceived by Marx makes normal political activity extremely difficult for it. To establish the proletarian hypothesis as a dominant factor in modern history, Marx originated, at least in embryo, a new kind of politics which went beyond agitational support of labor politics and a socialist critique of capitalism, as in *The Communist Manifesto* and *Capital*. To overcome the prolonged quiescence of the proletariat, he assigned to his theory the function of the material conditions in organizing proletarian consciousness and action —he sought *to create* the proletariat as a revolutionary class. Out of this effort to replace history arises Marxist politics, in which revolutionary unity and intelligence are born not from the pathetic experience of those who endure the situation but from the brain that has analyzed it.

As philosopher and historian Marx attacks the Utopians and "Marxists" for their dogmatism and their dreams of making history according to their plans; as a politician he himself is a Marxist. The intuition of history as a tragedy which, with the elimination of mythic collectivities, will terminate in a saving catastrophe is submerged under a programmatic optimism. With its action centered in the Marxist organization, the proletariat seems to shed its hypothetical character. An appearance of moving toward the socialist goal relieves the workers of their awful, pathetic choice between permanent revolution and nothingness. In time the human "recoil" before the "indefinite prodigiousness" of socialist revolution ceases to play any part in the writings of the movement (except with Georges Sorel and Rosa Luxemburg), or is used as a justification for various forms of Party discipline.

But having translated class consciousness from tragic self-recognition into political tutoring, Marxism is haunted by its philosophical premises. If the Marxian program constitutes the consciousness of the socialist revolution, whose existence determines that consciousness? That of the class? Or of the Party? Or is it an undetermined (free) manifestation of genius? So long as Marx could say, "The great social measure of the Commune [which was not a Marxist creation] was its own working existence," it was clear that theory was subordinate to the action of the class, and that Communist ideas were in truth attempting to be the intelligence of "the real movement that abolishes the present state of things." Once, however, class spontaneity has yielded to marching at the heels of the Party, the latter must look to itself as the source of historical consciousness, since it alone experiences history, while the masses are undergoing the "long, persistent work" of learning. But if its own existence guides it, the Marxist Party is "an independent being," that is, an illusory force, and its theory a mere ideology or a theology.* In that case the high claims of socialism that the "self-activity" of the proletariat would release all human individuals into unlimited creativity are no longer legitimate. Those claims rested upon the origin of the collective act in history itself, in the response of individuals to their common situation, rather than, as formerly, in a fiction or ideal; but now socialism has produced its own illusory community and independently existing creation of the mind.

Thus in the heart of Marxism a conflict rages between metaphysics (existence determines consciousness and defeats all preconceptions) and politics ("We can initiate measures"). The attempt to resolve this conflict through a "dialectical" combination of the messianism of total libera-

* The mark of an "ideologist," says Engels, is that "every act, since it is transmitted by thought, also seems to him in the last analysis to be *founded* on thought." Is not the aim of Party instruction that every act of the workers shall be *founded* on Marxism?

tion with discipline of the masses as an "army" can only result in a politics of hallucination. Marx's "we can initiate measures which will later appear as spontaneous movements" reveals the spuriousness of the synthesis of class spontaneity and ideological control. In this proposal a new principle has made its appearance. It is neither the materialist principle of the primacy of existence nor the idealist one that action has its source in thought. It is the mythical principle that action can release a foreseen destiny which both dominates existence and precedes thought. With the affirmation of this power, we stand at the verge of twentieth-century political irrationalism.

In Marxism first appears those deliberately created collective historical actors that have carried out the great social upheavals of our time. Primarily, this form of "destiny politics" consists of a demonic displacement of the ego of an historical collectivity (class, nation, race) by a Party of action, so that the Party motivates the community and lays claim to identity with its fate and to its privileges as a creature of history. Lenin* begins by denying that the proletariat can be an independent historical actor; for him the class is a collective character with a role but without the revolutionary ego and consciousness necessary to play its part. Its struggles are but reflexes of economic contradictions which can never of themselves rise to the level of revolution. The giant figure of the proletariat is doomed to remain a personification of exploitation and misery until it is possessed by a separately formed self that will send it hurtling along its predestined path. This conscious, active ego is the Bolshevik Party of "scientific" (destiny-knowing) professional revolutionaries. The Party's relation to the class is demoniacal in the most literal sense; after a series of paroxysms the body of the class is inhabited and

* In *What Is to Be Done?*

violently moved by an independent will which is that of another group or even of one man. For Lenin the word "subjectivity" means precisely the Party and its decisions.

If the revolutionary violence of the proletariat resulted from its historical situation, the individuals of the class could bear no moral responsibility—it will be recalled that Marx accorded to the capitalists, too, immunity from class guilt. The class exists "outside" the individual and compels him; while its own acts are necessary in the sense that necessity exists in the physical world. Even if the class were responsible, who could judge it? Only history itself, whose creature and "agent" it is. "History is the judge," says Marx, "the proletariat its executioner." Hence so long as its hero is actually the revolutionary working class Marxism need not concern itself with the morality of its means —the truth itself, through which the instinctive response of the victim-hero is transformed into a conscious act, is its sole and exclusive means.

Political Marxism claims for its own organized will the metaphysical privileges of class action. The violence of the "vanguard," having become "dialectically" the act of the proletariat, justifies itself by the existence of the workers as victims of the capitalist wage system. Any attack by Marxist professionals becomes by definition a liberating movement against the system on the part of the class. Thus the Party need not account for the means it employs—all the more so since its program is held to be identical with the reality from which all future moral values will spring. Bolshevism has even denied that the form of its organization is a "principled question"—in it, total autocracy is not inconsistent with total democracy, since the acts of the Party are the acts of the proletariat and the proletariat is, again by definition, the demos.

As it attributes to the class the subjectivity of the Party, without regard to the actual will or consciousness of the workingman, so too it attributes a hostile subjectivity—that is, evil intentions—to the "embodiments of particular class interests." Capitalists and peasants are held automatically guilty of historical crimes, in disregard of the unwillingness of Marx to "make the individual responsible for relations whose creatures he socially remains." This practice of bringing social categories artificially to life is the root of Marxian terrorism.

Morally bewildered by assuming for itself the role of the class, the Party alter ego destroys by the same means the basis for historical insight which was the genius of Marx. The Party pretends to analyze events in class terms; standing in the place of the proletariat it can see only itself. Traditional parties are aware that they represent specific configurations of interests and beliefs. The Marxist Party of action does not feel itself *in the presence of* any social body. To it, the featureless mass of laborers exists historically only as the Party has created it; the Party program is imposed as the only true expression of the workers' interests, and their own demands are errors that must be eliminated. The Party is an absolute with regard to the class, and through it an absolute with regard to history. Referring to the "lag" of workers behind the Party of the most advanced, Engels asserts: "and this alone explains why it is that actually the 'solidarity of the proletariat' is everywhere realized in different party groupings which carry on life and death feuds with one another, as the Christian sects in the Roman Empire did amidst the worst persecutions." *

Thus, as a liberating program Marxist politics founders on the issue of the subjectivity of the proletariat. So soon as Marxism declares its own conception of events, rather than the common situation of men, to be the inspiration of revo-

* In a letter to Bebel, 1873.

lutionary unity and ardor, Marxism becomes an ideology competing with others. When fascism derided the revolutionary working class as the invention of Marxism, it was but repeating the secret idea, of the Marxist parties themselves. Once the class became in practice a mere physical extension of the Party, the future could be decided by a magical contest in creating mass egos. In this contest, fascism demonstrated that heroic pantomime, symbolism, ritual, mass bribery, appeals to the past and to fantasy could overwhelm ideological class consciousness. The choice for the workers became one between the Fascist costume drama and a socialism that urged them to regard their own work clothes as a costume. In Germany and Italy the working class was driven off the stage of history by the defeat of the Party—in Russia it was driven off by its victory.

The elimination of the illusory community has proved to be far more difficult than Marx imagined. Though largely released from religious mythology, the consciousness of the workingmen has not become an infallible reflection of their bare material condition. Nor has the pastless barbarism of the modern psyche immunized it to heroes and abstract beliefs. In moments of crisis the new-fangled men seem as susceptible to self-surrender as their tradition-haunted predecessors. They have neither chosen nor been compelled to change themselves into the inhuman "character assigned to them by the process of production."

Still, the proletarian personification remains. A uniform external character imposes itself upon the mass of wage workers. The presence of this mask continues *to imply* action on their part, no matter how many times the class shows itself to be in fact incapable of it. Neither theory nor events can refute the hypothesis of the revolutionary working class. *So long as the category exists,* the possibility cannot be excluded that it will recognize itself as a separate human community and revolutionize everything by asserting its needs and its traditionless interests.

In this proletarian category a unique power is concentrated. No modern government can survive against the expressed antagonism of its workers—decades ago Sorel pointed out that trading on the chances of that expression is the chief feature of contemporary politics. Whatever the flaws in the theory of history as an epic of class struggle, the potent effects in our time of the *likelihood* of class struggle cannot be denied. On the one hand, existing social orders are permanently menaced by the workers' tremendous potential power; on the other, the fact that this power rests with an anonymous category, an historical "nothing," tempts modern mythmakers to seize upon the working class as raw material for fictitious new collectivities by which society can be subjugated. Cannot the traditionless proletariat be converted into *anything* as readily as into itself? Keeping the drama in suspense between revolution by the working class on its own behalf and revolution as a tool for others, the pathos of the proletariat dominates modern history.

3

The Riddles of Oedipus

The central intuition of Greek tragedy, as of psychoanalysis, is: there is one unique fact which each individual anxiously struggles to conceal from himself, and this is the very fact that is the root of his identity.

Kierkegaard describes a type of despair in which the self "wills desperately to be itself—with the exception, however, of one particular, with respect to which it wills despairingly not to be itself."

Action is heroic when, in addition to displaying courage, fidelity, etc., it involves an overcoming of this automatic will to ignorance, when it reverses the inner process that repels the one particular and forces the actor to embrace it.

Tragedy is the willful movement toward the hidden fact by which the hero is identified. The hero does not know what his action will disclose but he is impelled toward the disclosure. The curtain rises at the moment when the process of revelation begins. A messenger arrives, an encounter takes place. It is the same in *Oedipus Tyrannus,*

Macbeth, Hamlet, Othello, Crime and Punishment. The first gesture begins to place the hero's apparent identity in question. Is he really a king, or a murdering parricide? Glamis, Cawdor or . . . ? Prince or clown? Hero or subman? *Hamlet* opens with "Who's there?" The first line of *Macbeth* after the witches' prelude is: "What bloody man is that?"

The hero is met with the Socratic demand: "Know thyself." In each instance, Man is also put into question—is *he* a king or a parricide, prince or clown? But the hero meets the demands of knowledge in terms of particular acts relating to himself, rather than by speculating about the human species. For the action is the point of the knowing, in that it partakes in creating, and makes itself responsible for, that which it brings to light. The tension of *Oedipus* arises from its hero's insistence on continuing the investigation as an aim to be fulfilled after its horrid findings have become as predictable as a result in mathematics. In action the disclosure of the self is an aspect of the self's coming into being—without the tragic or comic event of self-recognition, the self would not exist.

Hence the dramatic hero is always a hero of self-knowledge. Merely to dominate events without being taken by surprise by what one's acts unearth about oneself is to have missed the heroic. The history of mankind is filled with powerful personages empty of dramatic meaning.

Can the command, "Know thyself," be fulfilled through philosophy, or does it necessarily require action? The two riddles solved by Oedipus state what can be achieved by philosophy and what by action. First comes the riddle of the Sphinx, the "What-is-it-that . . . ?" riddle of philosophy. Then comes the riddle of Oedipus' individual being, the "Who-are-you . . . ?" riddle of tragedy.

The "What-is-it?" riddle put by the Sphinx of metaphysics could be solved by a generalization, and Oedipus slew this beast with the abstraction: Man. As Oedipus later boasted to Tiresias, he arrived at this reply through his own sagacity, not through divination; though perhaps he owed his genius for generalization to the fact that, having just slain his father, he thought of himself abstractly as Man rather than as a particular person—the deeper the crime one has to hide, the more abstract he tends to make himself.

At any rate, for his speculative triumph over the Sphinx, Oedipus was rewarded—given the kingdom of Thebes and its queen, and honored as a sage. He had run a deadly risk in going to meet the Sphinx. But it was a rational risk, in which one could win or lose. For the Sphinx slew only those who gave the *wrong* answer.

Existence, on the other hand, destroys those who give the right answer.

If philosophy could solve the problem of individual identity, the universal with which Oedipus replied to the Sphinx would have overpowered the evil design of the Fates. Since Oedipus knew what Man was, he should have been able to generalize his situation and to respond to it rationally, whatever it happened to be at the moment— one can imagine him explaining to his mother how absurd it would be to acknowledge personal guilt for the preordained. Had the slayer of the Sphinx mastered the secret of his own identity, or been able to liquidate his identity through philosophy, whatever he had done could be a step toward a happy ending, like the salvation of the Christian on his deathbed, or the restoration of the neurotic by psychoanalysis.

Solving the riddle of the Sphinx was, however, of no help to Oedipus—on the contrary, it led directly to his marriage with Jocasta. Philosophy, which at the beginning seemed so promising, not only failed Oedipus, it was responsible for his disaster. The riddle of the Sphinx led only to the second riddle, "Who are you?," which repeated the riddle of Man to Oedipus in terms of his own identity. This second riddle actually preexisted the first, since a man must be born before he is a man, and its content was the unique plot by which his existence was shaped: that he was doomed to slay his father and father children on his mother. In regard to this riddle philosophy was totally blind, and for arriving at the true answer to it Oedipus was destroyed.

The assumption of tragedy is that in actual life it is impossible to win, except by way of the destruction itself—and winning through being destroyed is not a rational risk but a transcendental hypothesis. Instead of the rewards that go to the abstract solver of problems, the payment for knowing oneself finitely, since it is a unique knowledge, and since it must be enacted in practice, is disgrace, banishment, death. Nations, classes also earn this tragic reward for stubbornly identifying themselves.

The hero suffers tragically for arriving at the right answer—in fact, only for the right answer. Through wrong answers Oedipus might have saved himself indefinitely, that is, until his false identity was destroyed by time. A wrong answer, one not leading to self-knowledge, may also bring misfortune, but the misery it causes, like that resulting from accident or lack of skill, is not tragic. The hero of a tragedy, however, cannot end with a wrong answer. For the tragedy begins in the revelation, when the possible wrong moves by which destiny can be averted have failed;

and the tragedy moves forward in the knowing; its action belongs to the revelation, as the hero belongs to his ignorance, and is hence necessarily accurate. As his deeds displace his will, leaving him less and less choice, they become identical with his consciousness in its not-to-be-deflected hunter's interest in his own being—the plot is *not* an infernal trap or machine which he continues to resist; it reflects the interest of thought in his fate, that is to say, in his election; and the deeper he enters into that plot, the greater the ecstasy of his yielding to the truth it is bringing into being.

The second solution of Oedipus was not to be given all at once in a word; it had to achieve its reality in unfinished acts, partial disclosures, false scents that led in the right direction. This time Oedipus does not arrive at the answer through his cleverness or wisdom—indeed, he contributes to the dénouement only through the persistence of his mistakes. The answer comes to Oedipus through the predictions, recollections, anxieties and evasions of his entire world—shepherds, messengers, Jocasta and so on. And this time the answer is not "Man" but "I," like the biblical prophet's "Here I am."

Oedipus begins as a young philosopher and ends as an old hero—contrary to the progress of knowledge from the particular to the universal. And his tragic unveiling affects not his ideas but his energies—the demolition of his false identity opens up tremendous springs of vitality in him, though this increase in his forces is experienced as anguish. Unlike philosophical knowledge, which Socrates concluded is a readiness to die, tragic knowledge sweetens life beyond the need for consolation. Before his torment began, Oedipus was ready to die—with a philosopher's readiness. Why else would he have risked his life on the Sphinx's riddle?

He was attracted to enigmas, was possessed by a sense of the concealed fact—in short, was an amateur of the hidden. Like Plato's cave philosopher he was dazzled by the invisible, and his hold on reality was weak—all of which is another way of saying that he offered no great resistance to death. While he was a philosopher Oedipus let himself drift toward destruction, because his self was hidden from him. But when his tragedy has been fulfilled and he has attained the full horror of self-recognition, he does not kill himself. No, he demands to live, with a fury that still amazes us; and this desire for life grows ever stronger in his blind and hopeless exile, as his intimacy with himself increases. So that in Colonus, Oedipus is infinitely grander and more powerful than he was as King of Thebes, and his passion for life is so immense that it propels him into immortality.

What makes psychoanalysis the opposite of tragedy, both as a form of knowledge and in its effect on the psyche, is that the sufferer hands over to another—the analyst—the process of disclosing who he is, instead of struggling toward self-knowledge through action. He makes himself passive in the expectation of being shown to himself as an object. The unwrapping of his ego will, he believes, relieve the misery of his self-estrangement. Solving puzzles cannot, however, as Oedipus learned, constitute a path to identity but, at best, only to a theoretical conception of Man. Thus the "cure" of the psychoanalytical patient actually consists in emptying him of individuality and rendering him more abstract—for example, he is given his share in the universal Jocasta through understanding how the Oedipus complex has affected him. The aboriginal fact by which he is identified is not brought to consciousness in a new enactment; instead, the fact has been dissolved mentally into the common formula. Because of its derivations from Greek mythology psychoanalysis believes it can open up the life-giving springs of tragic catharsis, but in practice the energizing fails to occur because of the inevitable abstractness of the psychoanalytical experience.

Those who speak of the tragedy of history conceive human collectivities as undergoing a process of identity-disclosure analogous to that of individuals. For Marx society is made up of several class identities in conflict with one another; each of these arrives at itself through a revolutionary enactment which transforms both its own existence and that of the historic whole in which it functions. Thus the Paris Commune, the first attempt of the proletariat to affirm itself as an independent collective entity, is termed a tragedy by Marx; while the attempt of French middle-class society to transcend itself through the false heroics of Louis Bonaparte is treated by Marx as a case of mistaken identities, hence a farce. That class identity is the central fact of contemporary social behavior is suggested by the incessant efforts of all modern societies, including those which have given the Marxist answer to the Sphinx (that is, Man, the worker), to conceal the class "I" in action under such substitute identities as Nation, Race, Party, Cult. For if the class identity is the true, active social persona of the world's laboring masses, it is by that fact the source of a slow, tragic undermining of existing realities, and society, including the working class itself, cannot experience the struggle of the new class to affirm itself without suffering the destructive consequences of solving the second riddle, that is, of discovering who this anonymous mass is. The moment the hidden name is called the wheels of tragedy begin to turn, the subjective being of each social class rises toward relentless self-expression, and the effort toward knowledge becomes a battle for survival.

The dramatic problem of the twentieth century is that of

the relation between collective identities active on the stage of history and the self of the individual as a more or less willing component of a mass "I." If a social group is actually a "being" which becomes engaged in the tragic process of self-knowledge regardless of the volition or intelligence of its individual members, the traditional concept of individual existence is put into question. History is *the* tragic spectacle—one in which everybody is at once a member of the cast and of a captive audience forced to become conscious of the unfolding of events. Yet the life interest of the individual remains his interest in knowing himself. Mass and individual actions are rival modes of self-knowledge that give rise to new dramatic forms.

"Know thyself" is the link between philosophy and drama, as "Suppress thyself" is the link between philosophy and science. In drama everything moves toward the repetition in consciousness of the unique identifying fact. First this fact is known to the Oracle, then to Oedipus in terms of mistaken identities and false moves, then it is realized through his action, then in his consciousness of his action, finally, in his transformation as the consequence of this consciousness and the reversal of his situation. The spiraling of events that establishes identity provides the content of individual existence.

Scientific thinking moves in the opposite direction—toward experiences that can be duplicated experimentally and toward questions for which anyone can supply the right answer. The urge of the individual to self-repetition is in the view of science an atavism grounded in the blindness of self-love.

The problem of individual identity is the dilemma of philosophy. If philosophy attempts to deal with the single individual, it tends in the direction of action and beyond the border of generalization: it is forced to merge its thinking into art or into religion. If, on the other hand, philosophy excludes the individual in order to harmonize its methods with those of science, it cannot reach the individual except, as Kierkegaard points out, in a footnote; which means that philosophy replies to the question of "Who?" with an ethic of adjustment by which the individual is trimmed to fit the needs of some social or moral scheme without regard to what he might discover about himself as a unique being.

In Plato, "adjustment" is represented by the vision of harmony between the right and left horses of spirit. But despite Plato's so-called anti-tragic outlook, his ideal of rational self-curtailment is ironically contradicted by the dramatic image of Socrates, who embodies, fulfills and surpasses the theoretical presuppositions of virtue; who knows himself by "a species of madness," as well as by speculating about man; who grounds knowledge in recollection and the act of thinking in love; who, in a kind of exemplary self-temptation, lets loose and even encourages in himself the passions which are to be held in check; and who, by the manner of his death for "giving the right answer," demonstrates that the act of knowing must be completed tragically. It seems an essential presupposition of Plato's thought that philosophy tends toward the dramatic, that it develops its concepts through the conflicting notions of specific human beings, and that hence the dialogue, which is speculation within the mold of individual behavior and itself a mode of behavior, is the necessary form of philosophy. Through the dialogue and its actors, Plato attempts to overcome the dilemma of philosophy in the face of individual identity.

In the dialogue each speaker is a living hypothesis. He asserts himself and his ideas absolutely; but since his statements presuppose a listener, each statement actually begins: "Assuming that I am I and that humanity is like me, such and such is the case." It is impossible for a thinker in a dialogue to present himself as Philosophy. Kierkegaard argues that Socrates' very existence is hypothetical: "On this 'if' [of immortality] he risks his entire life, he has the courage to meet death, and he has with the passion of the infinite so determined the pattern of his life that it must be found acceptable—if there is an immortality."

When philosophy abandons the dialogue, when it becomes the voice of a single speaker, it cannot avoid asserting an absolute. By putting his name on the title page of his work, the philosopher declares that the "I" by which he is known is truly he, and that the truth known to this "I" can be the truth for all. Assuming that this claim is justified, the reader has become a tenant of the author's world, and this is the case even when the single, unhypothetical speaker is a purely instrumental thinker. The concealed teleology of instrumentalism, like that of any other non-dramatic philosophy, is that humanity is an instrumentalist in different degrees of perfection; so there is ideological effort in it to transform all men into Man.

It was clear to Kierkegaard that philosophy, when it does not voluntarily transcend itself in religion, ought to be many-voiced, that one should speak as oneself only with respect to the religious. Reasserting Plato's principle of philosophy as drama, he used pseudonyms for those of his works which were not sermons, and underlined the point by writing dialogues signed with pseudonyms. That Kierkegaard's disguises as an author were so thin indicates that he used them less to cover his identity before the public than as a sign that an author had to be another. In place of the self-suppression of the philosopher of knowledge for the sake of the universal, the philosopher of identity practices self-concealment as a token that he cannot speak for himself. He denies himself not in order to hide, but because his self *is* hidden; it is still to be arrived at, and the very aim of his thinking lies, as Kierkegaard says, in "becoming subjective," that is, himself.

But this becoming subjective is an activity that can be ended only by death: "The very point is that it should last for a whole life." Self-concealment represents the fact that at any given moment the thinker's identity has still to be attained. So the pseudonym is the signature of his faith, an avowal of the unknown and that it is always present. It is his means of affirming the other self both as a reality and as a possibility—but this affirmation is made negatively through declaring his visible, active self to be a disguise.

Hamlet, or What Shall I Become? The Despair of Dramatic Philosophy

Considering the pseudonymous author of dramas and dialogues, a concealed philosopher holding back from the absolutes of religion and throwing forth fictions like a film projector, distributing himself into a cast of characters among whom he himself may not appear, one thinks at once of Hamlet instructing the players—how easy it is to act as an actor, so long as one does not have to act as oneself. But this thinker knows that direct affirmation of the self is impossible, since every form of action, even that of music or dance, is an estrangement.

Kierkegaard develops the incommunicability of the self, distinguishing this condition from the play acting of the modern snob of deep feeling. "Now he has even succeeded in obtaining town criers of inwardness, and a town crier of inwardness is quite a remarkable species of animal."

Since communication of the self is impossible except

through approximation and hints, the philosopher of identity is driven to dramatic fiction. On the stage he can exchange his tentative self for a definite part, and thus desist from pursuing the unattainable "Who" by making himself over into a "That." On the stage, too, he can enact experimentally, and with reduced risk, the events by which he supposes himself to be identified, as Hamlet did in his play within the play, and thus approach the truth.

But while through drama the philosopher of self could keep the game going, he is drawn away from drama in the direction of religion, for drama leads him only to endless hypostatization, while through faith he may succeed in completing his actual self with the experience of God. For Kierkegaard, edifying works may be signed with one's own name.

Thus the pseudonymous philosopher, finding consciousness of his own identity to be beyond his capacities, is tempted to transform himself either into an actor or into a mystic; at the same time he is aware that to become either is to surrender, and that it is his obligation as a conscious individual to keep trying to realize the incommunicable in action. This mixture of desire for a role and fear of being trapped in a role constitutes the peculiar malady out of which arises modern action philosophy, with its dream of revolutionizing the metaphysical condition of man. Kierkegaard speaks of reading Hegel "in the light of action." But though for the action philosopher truth lies in doing, he retains his tie with philosophy in that he understands the aim of action to be the affirmation of identity in the consciousness and not merely the achievement of objective ends, as with the utilitarians. To discover the beginning of a self the actor must conceive his acts as experiments and keep his mind alert for clues as to which of these experiments might apply to him. In his dramatic laboratory any act is the potential originator of an identity more firmly defined than that of the author. One has only to move into the track of consequence and a life will be fatally structured. Here choice is the origin of existence, and the doer must be infinitely cautious.

Hence standing in the center of a vibrating field of possibility, the pseudonymous philosopher tends to refrain from action and suspend himself in the imaginary, that is, verbal action. Whatever he might do would be the deception of an actor; the worst self-deception would consist in favoring the actor whom he originally found masquerading in his image. All selves are equally justified; and "the self," said Kierkegaard, "despairingly wills to dispose of itself or to create itself, to make itself the self it wills to be, distinguishing in the concrete self what it will and will not accept." Kierkegaard could make himself into Don Juan or into Aesthete and be in accord with every word that each uttered. But to begin with himself was not even thinkable, except on the hypothesis of the religious or tragic "leap."

The dramatic philosopher's condition of suspension prior to the start of an action is, by the testimony of Hamlet and Kierkegaard, a condition of despair, the poetic despair of possibility without reality. No matter how passionate, how reasonable, how humanly sympathetic his behavior may be, it produces only momentary satisfaction, since it fails to bring him closer to self-realization. His good and his evil are as if performed for the benefit of an audience. Kierkegaard describes this despair of possibility:

If the despairing self is active, it really is related to itself only as experimenting with whatsoever it be that it undertakes, however great it may be, however astonishing, however persistently carried out . . . in the last resort it lacks seriousness . . . every instant it can quite arbitrarily begin all over again, and however far a thought may be pursued, the whole action is within a hypothesis. It is so far from being true that the self succeeds more and more in becoming itself, that in fact it merely becomes more and more manifest that it is a hypothetical self.

The anguish of possibility is dramatized when the individual's situation is partly disclosed as a riddle which he can guess at, rather than as a set of circumstances prompting him to act. Hamlet learns how his father died, but this knowledge only multiplies his notions about himself. Similarly, a university professor discovers that his wife has been unfaithful to him, and this leads to his reinterpreting the facts in his memory to picture himself as a voyeur, or as a latent homosexual or as an intellectual sadist. Given his half-darkened situation, Hamlet experiments: he acts in order to bring about a disclosure, as if he were adding a chemical to a mixture, rather than to achieve a concrete result. His primary aim is to undermine the foundations of his life to date, in order to open the way to a new choice of roles; so that "quite arbitrarily," in Kierkegaard's phrase, he keeps questioning himself as if he were at a beginning. The reality of Hamlet as a character, in contrast to the usual order of dramatic fictions, is his desire for an aesthetic suspension, for the non-identity of his author. He stops for as long as he can in self-negation (Kierkegaard's "first movement of resignation").

Though Kierkegaard experienced the "renunciation of everything" after his love affair with Regina, he cannot be compared with Hamlet. Under the pressure of the plot the latter was forced to act; while Kierkegaard, suffering precisely from the absence of a "plot" in real life, remained a philosopher free to "make the movements" of resignation and faith, that is to say, to escape his situation by shadow actions of spirit. "Love," he says in *Fear and Trembling* about the lover resigned to the loss of his "princess," "became for him the expression for an eternal love, assumed a religious character, was transfigured into a love for the Eternal Being." This power of religion to do away with a fact does not exist in drama, where the hero is chained to his part; nor does it exist in the actual world, where the fact refuses really to be transfigured, as Kierkegaard so thoroughly explained in his psychological studies.

Kierkegaard accepted the Christian promise of salvation as *the* fact of human life, though he puts it to the extremest test of practice, from which it emerged as salvation "by virtue of the absurd." Salvation breaks across the Greek idea of tragedy and self-knowledge—in this vital respect, Christianity, like science, is the antagonist of drama, that is, of self-knowledge through action. To be saved means to have completed the partly disclosed self in the universality of God's commandments, to have moved away from the given condition of identity toward the "God-relation" in order to avoid pursuing the action to its conclusion. The Christian as Christian completes himself in the infinite; if he suffers it is because of the inadequacy of his faith. Thus a medieval Christian writer was quite logical when he wrote that Jesus could have forgiven the crime of Oedipus. In Christian thought the identifying fact is conceived as sin, which may be wiped away by divine mercy, as psychoanalysis wipes it away through steeping it in abstractions. Tragic action thus loses its function of concrete self-knowledge, and Oedipus appears not as a hero but as the victim of a meaningless arrangement of chance happenings. If individual identity is synonymous with sin, the only wisdom is to escape from senselessness and misery into an order of abstract ideas, that is, to renounce the second riddle of Oedipus.

Kierkegaard is the theoretician (as Dostoyevsky is the dramatist) of the despair of possibility without reality—that condition of modern man, who can no longer believe and who yet cannot acknowledge that he is a mere item in a system of abstract processes. Since he is not bound to anything given, he is capable of playing countless roles, but only as an actor, that is, with the consciousness that he has assumed a disguise. (If the disguise proves to be permanent, he will have trapped himself by his choice; if it is not permanent, he will have wasted his time in it and nullified a portion of his life.) The exchangeability of the fiction which he has become constitutes a degree of freedom never before attained by man in the mass. But it is the freedom to put on an act, for others and for oneself—the protagonist of Dostoyevsky's *A Raw Youth* is able to see himself simultaneously as a billionaire and as a St. Jerome in his cave.

The individual, however, is not content to be an actor. That there is no "I" that he will find at the bottom of his being is itself the "one particular" about which he continues to delude himself. It is his fixed belief in his ultimate identity that makes him a mimic of forms—and one who feels falsified by form. This is another way of saying that modern man is, ultimately, an aesthete—one whose highest ideal is not the good but a self constructed according to a model of "the most beautiful man," Socrates, for example, or Christ, or some revolutionist clothed in the glamour of the times.

4

The Stages:
Geography of Action

> ". . . A speech . . . which I would insert and set down in't."
>
> *Hamlet*

> "Everybody wants to get into the act."
>
> <small>JIMMY DURANTE</small>

PRELUDE—*The Gravedigger as Cultural Historian*

Each time the spade strikes into the ground another skull is turned up. Why is the graveyard so crowded? Because Denmark is a small country? Rather because the world is a stage, and a stage is a structure for putting on temporary displays, so there is no storage space. "Elsinore: A platform." Everything is on or near the surface. All that horseplay about "lugging the guts" of Polonius about.

> ROSENCRANTZ: Where the dead body is bestow'd, my lord,
> We cannot get from him.

Hamlet has hidden the corpse somewhere, but it is bound to show up again. The actors who leave this lighted box can only depart under the floor, where each burrows among the offstage mob to get as close as he can to the scene over-head. "You hear this fellow in the cellarage?"

Dig and there are skulls. Stick a sword through a wall that is a curtain and a voice will cry out, "I am slain!" So many bodies packed near the sides and underfoot no thrust can fail to land. Those ejected from the scene struggle to return to it. They have no place else to go. Hades is closed; also heaven and hell. This lighted rectangle is all there is. The actor whose part is finished goes to where he will be seen no more.

The stage which is the world floats in an ether of long-ing—the longing of the dead for one more performance. The longing of dead Caesar, the longing of dead Yorick.

The hero is he who has the power to return to the stage after he has been carried off—the power to be resurrected. He holds himself in readiness in the darkness, until events happening above give him his cue to break forth again into the light.

If there were another stage, above or below, for those who are finished here, some camp of the dead in which they could endlessly repeat their stories, like those sighing histo-ries heard by Odysseus, the stage of present action would not be so besieged by players of obsolete episodes.

Since, however, the visible stage is all, a void appears at the end of each man's performance, as the abyss at the end of the sea appeared before the fifteenth-century mariner.

Once this void has been sensed, how desperately the actor clings to the one stage! For he knows that the time will come when he will be driven from it forever. Then he will be turned to nothingness.

So a new ontological anxiety appears: the anxiety to get into the act—and to remain in it as long as possible. Also to make sure that the part one plays will really be one's own.

I

The world is a stage and one is compelled to act, but one's actions are no longer imposed from above, and each living person is aware that he has something within himself which is more real than the part assigned to him by events. Hamlet is obsessed by the sense of being an actor, that is to say, of falsifying himself through what he does and says. His self-consciousness exceeds his role and blocks his performance of it.

This is another way of saying that Shakespeare has put aside the conventions of the theater in order to bring to the stage the imitation of an actual person. He has recast an old plot in terms of a realistic metaphysics—in the new theater not only must the deeds of the actors be shown but their state of being when they are not in action.

In *Hamlet,* being is separated from (is more than) doing. This separation is represented in Scene 1 by the apparition of the ghost. A ghost is a "character," but one incapable of action. He is an appearance out of the past, in this instance out of a time before the play began—in a word, a figure of history. He is helpless to affect events directly; he can only plead that others act for him. This soliciting of those presently on the stage by voices from the past is typical of the format of historical conflicts, and the first appearance of the ghost is immediately followed by Horatio's account of the wars and treaties between Denmark and Norway, and the current military crisis.

In bringing on the ghost as a key character, Shakespeare has turned drama for the first time toward the condition of the actor who exists even when he does not act, as in the case of a political leader whose role suddenly lapses because of a change in the situation. This newly revealed possibility of a gap between the actor and his action is the subject of *Hamlet*. Throughout the play, the issue of acting and of the deceptions of gesture and makeup is raised again and again as counterpoint to Hamlet's awareness of being in the drama of history, in which the actors are living beings and not fictions of the theater.

The nature of the new theater is raised in Act 1, Scene 2, in the first dialogue among the principals—Hamlet, his mother, King Claudius—none of whom is aware of the visit of the ghost.

> QUEEN: Good Hamlet, cast thy nighted colour off . . .
> Do not for ever with thy veilèd lids
> Seek for thy noble father in the dust.

Hamlet's part calls for wearing the costume of the dark off-stage and seeking his father in the ground. He keeps his head down, scanning the earth as if for a magical trap door to the world below. Hamlet does not know, as Odysseus did, where to find the dead. In Elsinore the ancient maps no longer apply. Yet Hamlet is acting on the assumptions of the old world, that those on stage can communicate with actors exiled from it.

Hamlet's belief that the actor may survive his part is op-posed by his mother on the ground that action must now be guided by practical experience. In seeking the dead, Hamlet violates the laws of nature.

> QUEEN: Thou know'st 'tis common; all that lives must die,
> Passing through nature to eternity.

Hamlet readily assents to Gertrude's generalization ("Ay, madam, it is common"), which is contradicted by his be-havior. He accepts the finality of death for all, though he has not accepted it for his father. His acquiescence draws the Queen into making the distinction of which he will take advantage. She attempts to force Hamlet to be logical:

> If it be,
> Why seems it so particular with thee?

Why does Hamlet imagine that in this one instance the actor will escape the nothingness of actors whose parts are finished? Hamlet's reply notes the contrast between the fictional existence of actors and the concreteness of individuals. In the new theater, the particularity of the human person is in conflict with the traditional structure of roles and appearances.

> HAMLET: Seems, madam! Nay, it is; I know not seems.

Yes, all men are mortal. And in the theater it is customary to deal with the typical, since the theater is an arena of illusions. But on this stage the particular is being affirmed in its opposition to the typical. Here a real person dies, not a fiction of one—and each man's death is particular to him and to those who love him. In the old theater the distinction between "is" and "seems" would have been meaningless; there seems and is were identical. But on the stage which is the world, only the particular is, and seems must be rejected.

Hamlet goes on to define himself as an actor who is a living man and to analyze the relations of man and actor.

> HAMLET: Seems, madam! Nay, it is; I know not seems.
> 'Tis not alone my inky cloak, good mother,
> Nor customary suits of solemn black,
> Nor windy suspiration of forc'd breath,—
> No, nor the fruitful river in the eye,
> Nor the dejected haviour of the visage,

Together with all forms, moods, shows of grief,
That can denote me truly. These, indeed,
   seem,
For they are actions that a man might play:
But I have that within which passeth show;
These but the trappings and the suits of woe.

The actions that a man might play, the illusionistic actions
of an actor, belong to what is common. Insofar as he is an
actor, Hamlet is playing his part by wearing a black suit,
sighing, looking sad. But the living man has "that within"
which cannot be played by an actor; it exceeds the stage; it
is an unused remainder of action. It is a particular which is,
and cannot be reached by seems. Hence the situation of the
man-actor is not wholly of the stage; it is linked to the dark
offstage, and to play his part in the sequence of real events
Hamlet must seek the dead. In introducing the dimension
of his hidden self, Hamlet has proclaimed that on the stage
which is the world the situation of the individual is not
that which he has in common with others, and to which he
responds by playing his part, but is unique and beyond appearances.

I I

The rejoinder to Hamlet comes from the actor who plays
the King. The criminal Claudius is a philosopher of man as
actor—he sees human existence as a frieze of gestures,
public and private. Even when he has been "frighted" by
Hamlet's dramatic "false fire" into facing the fact that on
this stage the actor is also an individual (in that, for example, his acts can be reflected back to him), Claudius can
only conceive himself as playing a part. The act's the thing;
the man slips into it as into a mold and remains in it forever.

CLAUDIUS: There [in heaven] is no shuffling, there the
action lies
In his true nature.

Since the action that defines him is his murder of his
brother, Claudius seeks to disengage himself from his crime
and recover his innocence. He is the most pious character
in the play. He shows no remorse, but he would like to
clean the slate.

CLAUDIUS: O limèd soul, that, struggling to be free,
Art more engag'd!

But how to begin anew in the same situation?

. . . since I am still possess'd
Of those effects for which I did the murder.

Perhaps by a change of style—salvation of the actor.

. . . heart with strings of steel,
Be soft as sinews of the new-born babe!—
All may be well.

It is this actor's outlook, which calls for accommodating
one's feelings to one's part, that Claudius has urged upon
Hamlet as a wise yielding to necessity.

CLAUDIUS: For what we know must be, and is as common
As any the most vulgar thing to sense,
Why should we, in our peevish opposition,
Take it to heart?

Hamlet's desire to "denote me truly" becomes peevish re-
bellion against his assigned part.

CLAUDIUS: Fie! 'tis a fault to heaven,
A fault against the dead, a fault to nature,
To reason most absurd; whose common theme
Is death of fathers . . .

The human "that within" is but a distortion of the actor, says Claudius. Hamlet should cease his absurd and irrational opposition, accept the common theme of death and "think of us [Claudius] as a father." Performers, Claudius is arguing, are after all replaceable.

Claudius and Hamlet oppose each other in their conception of the stage and of the actor. To the King the situation is clear: he knows "what must be," and in the must be the actor prevails. To Hamlet the situation is a mystery, with a grief that passes show and which no action will affect.

III

The key to the choice between Claudius's "This must be so" and Hamlet's particular, "which knows not seems" is the ghost. In the absence of the ghost, Claudius must conquer. Were the dead actually finished, Hamlet's persisting in his search for his father would be an act of madness, a psychological aberration that distorts what is undeniable. All that is disappears, says life on the stage, your father is gone. A new situation has arisen—act in it. And Hamlet seems to turn away and hide from what he knows is the case. So his feeling that his loss is unique is an emotional self-indulgence, a fault that removes him from the human condition.

That the dead father actually appears completely alters the significance of Hamlet's passionate stubbornness. The father is entitled to demand revenge, but the hero cannot grasp the situation without communicating with the off-stage world. This in itself is sufficient to cut down the pace of the drama and inflect it toward meditation. Hamlet's grief that passes show, as the internal clue that the part he is playing is inadequate, becomes a force pushing him toward the unknown truth. The emotion that cannot be enacted reaches toward the actor who cannot be seen. Hamlet's rejection of what everyone knows is neither gratuitous rebelliousness nor the effect of psychological disorder; it is a tentative recognition of the true state of affairs. This recognition is confirmed by the return of the dead father to the stage. Once the existence of the ghost has been established, what is happening on the stage cannot be isolated from movements in those other, darkened areas—an accurate conception of the situation must now include the stage and the offstage, what is being played and what has been played, what cannot be enacted and what cannot be enacted yet but will be enacted in the future. Subjective, objective, unknown—Hamlet's inexpressible passion, the seeming of the actor, the impotence of the dead, all are dimensions of each moment of this history.

Thus, far from retreating from the situation, as he is accused of doing by his mother and Claudius, Hamlet has penetrated to its center through his double performance of seeking his father as a mourner while denying that his costume and his gestures truly represent his feelings. It is through such doubling and self-contradiction that the actor who is a man defines himself on the stage that is the world.

Having divined the inexpressibility of the particular, Hamlet cannot accommodate himself to the objective situation outlined for him by the determinist Claudius. But why not break out of his contradictions by acting at once in emulation of the ready Fortinbras,

> Whose spirit with divine ambition puffed
> Makes mouths at the invisible event?

Hamlet needs no ghost to supply him with a motive for attacking Claudius. He has sufficient political motive: to remove the man who "stands in the way of my election." Beyond this, he has a driving psychological impulse: hatred for the uncle who induced his mother

> . . . to post
> With such dexterity to incestuous sheets.

He has noted these "causes" from the start—why does he need to track down the invisible event instead of making mouths at it?

The contrast between Hamlet and Fortinbras has for centuries tempted critics to interpret *Hamlet* in terms of the psychological incapacity of its hero for the leap into action. In this light the play becomes a drama of weakness. Yet what forbids Hamlet to follow his impulse is not psychology but the structure of his situation. He is held to the individual seeking as well as to the actor's playing by the dead father to whom the "that within" has called and who has replied by appearing. Fortinbras can plunge into the future as if it were totally new. But Hamlet can satisfy his soul only to the extent that his act continues the invisible event that resulted in the murder of his father. In a word, Hamlet must act historically.

Marx perceived the encirclement of the living by the dead, and he spoke of the "conjuring up" of dead heroes as a phenomenon that accompanies all revolutions. When man has been driven to the depths of his situation, when his crisis has become absolute and he is forced to choose the unknown, his act cannot be his act alone; it takes place, says Marx, "in circumstances directly found, given and transmitted from the past." The new act arrives at the invisible event and joins itself to it. The dead are called on stage and the actors discover themselves to be henchmen of buried heroes. History becomes, in Marx's Shakespearean words, "a nightmare on the brain of the living."

The intervention of the dead inspires the actor's will at the same time that it illuminates the obstacles to action imposed by his individual situation. Before he can become one with his role, Hamlet must settle his relations with Ophelia and his mother. His consciousness of the density of the particular reaches the point of desperation.

> O, that this too too solid flesh would melt,
> Thaw, and resolve itself into a dew!

If he too could become a ghost the event would complete itself.

IV

Real situations are open at both ends—the actors do not know the circumstances, nor do they know themselves. Only on the mythical Other Stage, where legend, religion, art has set individuals into an invented plot of "What we know must be," can man and actor, being and role, become identical. Between the actor and the act that will denote him truly stands the intangibility of the particular. Hamlet with his "I know not seems" will continue to be pressed toward action but doomed never to begin.

> But break my heart, for I must hold my tongue.

Unless a moment arrives when the two invisible termini of the situation, the dead who cannot be seen and the "that within" which cannot be enacted, touch each other across the stage. Then a lightning consciousness of the entirety of the event will start the movement toward resolution. Hamlet's encounter with the ghost is such a beginning. In it the dust of the past replies to the questing anguish. Out of this communion arises the resolution "to pursue this act."

By indicating the possibility of a true act, the ghost transforms Hamlet's mood and his conception of conditions on this stage. Before, there were only the "weary, stale, flat and unprofitable . . . uses of this world . . . an unweeded garden, that grows to seed," possessed by "things rank and gross in nature . . . merely." The actor could only reflect his existence; he was powerless to change it. The ghost brought the promise of creative novelty into the world.

HORATIO: O day and night, but this is wondrous strange!
HAMLET: And therefore as a stranger give it welcome.

V

From the ghost Hamlet learned that it would be his part to complete the drama of his father's murder. This knowledge made a true act possible, but it also made it infinitely difficult. For Hamlet had to kill Claudius in a way that would appease the ghost.

The ghost supplied Hamlet with a profound motive deeper than ambition or jealousy. But revenge as a motive has a peculiar character. Ambition or hatred anticipates a result that will satisfy the actor. Revenge, in contrast, turns toward the past and must compensate the original victim. It seeks to bring about the equivalent of an event that has happened, in order to cancel it. For ambition or jealousy any slaying of Claudius would have been sufficient. But not for revenge. The offense of Claudius would not be balanced by *any* slaying. With the ghost's tale ringing in his ears, Hamlet had to conceive how his attack on the murderer could constitute a proper conclusion to the plot that had suddenly unfolded itself. He had to "write" the last act of the play he was in. In this again he found himself dedicated to the particular. His deed of revenge had to be aesthetically apt, a part perfectly fitted into the whole.

So when Hamlet stands behind Claudius as he kneels in prayer and can "do it pat," he rejects his opportunity with the exclamation, "And so am I reveng'd. That would be scann'd." And later he begs the ghost not to make him weep, lest through passion "what I have to do will want true colour."

Had the ghost never appeared, Hamlet might have slain Claudius much sooner—the more superficial the motive, the easier it is to act. But the slaying would have been an "action that a man might play," that is, a mere performance. Both statements relate to the arts.

To carry out a slaying that would be embedded in true color within the total situation, perfectly matching the hue of Claudius's crime, Hamlet had to overcome the contradiction between the actor and the man. His act would fit the event only if it responded to the circumstances as he found them; yet it had to be performed as an act of free choice. On the one hand, the hero must abandon himself to direction by the plot; on the other, he must consciously will his deed as an expression of his own self. Unless he is moved from the outside, he must wait; he cannot wait, for he is responsible. Hamlet promises to obey "thy commandment," a commandment that requires confirmation, yet "all occasions do inform against" him and spur his revenge. Thus he must become passive for the sake of action, mystified for the sake of exactness, a "dull and muddy-mettled rascal" in order to play the role of hero. Wearing the costume of the offstage night, he cannot say "I" unless the situation says it for him, he cannot decide unless it is decided. As the ghost fades, Hamlet takes leave of his friends:

HAMLET: I hold it fit that we shake hands and part:
         You, as your business and desire shall point you,
         For every man hath business and desire,
         Such as it is;—and, for mine own poor part,
         Look you, I will go pray.

The division within Hamlet extends to everything he sees. Words divide from their "matter," thought from its meaning, the appearance from the thing. His senses sharpened by his concentrated listening at the edge of the void, Hamlet confronts a waxworks world of false faces, stage sets and props, behind which lurk the business and desire of persons whose motives are hidden. Imprisoned in the unreal, he develops a mania for exposures. "God hath given you one face, and you make yourselves another." He keeps returning to the "counterfeit presentments" of life by art, at the same time that he finds life unendurable.

His assault on language is especially persistent. For language detached from the invisible event is the common tool of falsification.

POLONIUS: . . . What do you read, my lord?
HAMLET: Words, words, words.
POLONIUS: What is the matter, my lord? . . .
HAMLET: Slanders, sir: for the satirical rogue says here
        that old men have grey beards; that their faces
        are wrinkled . . . all of which, sir, though I
        most powerfully and potently believe, yet I
        hold it not honesty to have it thus set down.

What the "rogue" says is simple fact, yet the matter must be "scann'd" in the light of the author's motives. And in this light is it not plain that some hidden malice is at work? No doubt the writer whom Hamlet is reading is the enemy of some old man and is satirizing him by pointing to common characteristics of the aged. But these characteristics distort the image of the particular old man. For what is an old man? On the stage an old man is a mask with gray beard and wrinkles, "together with most weak hams." The satirical rogue is speaking of the mask. But "you yourself, sir, should be old as I am, if like a crab you could go backward." On the stage, time can be reversed as actors can be exchanged. Only in life do particulars exist and time move in a single direction; and it is not honesty to speak of an actual old man as if he consisted of a beard and wrinkles.

The platitudes concerning old men were false to their matter. Speaking of the ghost to Gertrude, Hamlet unveils a different use for language:

> Ecstasy!
> My pulse, as yours, doth temperately keep time,
> And makes as healthful music. It is not madness
> That I have utt'red: bring me to the test,
> And I the matter will re-word, which madness
> Would gambol from.

By "re-wording" the presence of the "bodiless creation" he would prove his sanity. His language would be an extension of the invisible, the genuine poetry of the seer—an initiation into a world in which the speaker plays his true part, as the things he describes are specimens of a clarified reality.

So Hamlet makes a distinction between words that serve the actor's falsification and those that unveil the invisible event. Guildenstern's phrases deserve contempt because they "would play upon" Hamlet and "pluck out the heart of [his] mystery." Osric is a clown because his speech and gesticulations "only got the tune of the time and outward habit of encounter." In contrast, Hamlet marvels at the gravedigger's verbal precision (he is one who digs under the stage): "How absolute the knave is!"

Hamlet itself is a "re-wording" of human action in the unknown situation. But it contains also the opposite, the rhetoric of drama as a tool, as in the play of the players—a thing to catch the King. In his instruction to the players Hamlet speaks of the drama as a perfect union of speech, action and meaning; and then he shows how a play can be falsified for a hidden end: "You could, for a need, study a speech of some dozen or sixteen lines, which I would set down, and insert in't, could you not?"

Everything that is not the act of true color is mere art to Hamlet, and art is an empty show with which to overcome an actor-adversary. The play keeps losing its hold on the actor who is a man. Hamlet's attempts to grasp his part are vitiated by passivity and endless calculation.

> Now, whether it be
> Bestial oblivion, or some craven scruple
> Of thinking too precisely on th' event,—
> . . . —I do not know
> Why yet I live to say, "This thing's to do;"
> Sith I have cause and will and strength and means
> To do't.

Like a figure by Rouault, Hamlet sits staring at a point in the distance from which all will be visible. Until Claudius sends him to England to be assassinated.

> HAMLET: Good.
> KING: So is it, if thou knew'st our purposes.
> HAMLET: I see a cherub that sees them.

VI

The two plays of the professional players brought to the stage by Hamlet are dream images of a kind of life in which the fatal rupture between being and action does not yet exist. The tryout of the death of Priam and the "play within the play" recall the earlier theater of clear-cut situations and unambiguous acts. They are projections of a myth world in which a man's actions represent him and leave no remainder. Hamlet's anguish as a dramatic misfit belonging to a time that is out of joint is conveyed by the contrast between his state and the direct reflexes of the players. The fact that these Other Stages are brought upon the visible stage, that they are made part of the action (the prime function of the Other Stage is to be a Place-for-Those-Who-Are-Not-Here), is an ironic assertion that man can no longer transcend his condition through dramatic fictions, that the age of absolute roles is at an end. Once the actor is conscious of the transformations wrought by myth, the power of myth is lost.

The healing magic of the Other Stage consists in the fact that there one knows his part and can give himself wholly to it. In the rehearsal of Aeneas' tale, the identity of man and actor is revealed in its antique form. The actor who weeps for Hecuba becomes the body of the part, his "whole function suiting." By the absoluteness of his acting, the player is transformed into a living personage beyond the "trappings" of his role. "Look," wonders Polonius enviously, "whe'er he has not turn'd his colour and has tears in 's eyes." Starting with his role the actor arrives at being—a movement from play acting to self. The antique actor corresponds, one might say, to Aristotle's man-the-political-animal, whose life is passed entirely under the eye of an audience (the community) and who, unconscious of any inexpressible "that within," achieves individual existence through the qualities of his social behavior.

The players' performance brings to the stage which is the world the dramatic equivalent of heaven and hell, an image of action without a human remainder, as in the order of the angels or the judged. Man suffers in the old tragedy—for example, the brutal "mincing" of old Priam —but his wounds are external and his pain arouses pity and fear. Hence Hamlet looks upon this scene with envy and compares the uninhibited passions of its performers with his own self "unpregnant of my cause." The identity of the actor and his act liquidates for the players the conflict by which Hamlet is torn. "Let those that play your clowns speak no more than is set down for them." It is as if Hamlet offered himself as a model of what to avoid—let not the performer exceed his part.

VII

The stage is surrounded by the dead, and on it the actor is in conflict with himself as a man. The play of the players is put on in a circle of light, beyond which sit the spectators, themselves actors—that is to say, in the play within the play there is only acting and no residue of individual being.

> KING: What do you call the play?
> HAMLET: *The Mouse-trap.*

The Mouse-trap is a parody of the antique theater in which the act is all. The players are trapped by their audience; audience and players are trapped in a fiction; and the play is put on to trap the King, one of the actor-spectators. The play reflects back to Claudius his philosophy of man as an actor who when his hour on the stage is ended disappears forever.

As *The Mouse-trap* opens, the Player King, speaking in cyclical metaphors of the passage of time (as repetition, not as duration), anticipates his own death. When this occurs, he foresees that he will be replaced and the action will go on as before. ("And thou shalt live in this fair world behind.") Death is simply a termination of activity. It comes when "My operant powers their functions leave to do." Repeating the view of Claudius regarding the attitude that Hamlet ought to assume toward his dead father, the Player King advises his Queen to prepare to continue her act with another husband.

The Player Queen interrupts him by reciting Hamlet's inserted lines. In her rejoinder to Claudius's "What we know must be," Hamlet's mouthpiece changes the concept of necessity into an accusation of crime. To replace her dead husband, she declares, would amount to murdering him—indeed, to murdering him twice.

> PLAYER QUEEN: A second time I kill my husband dead,
> When second husband kisses me in bed.

Hamlet has made her say that accepting death as a necessity means in human terms to keep destroying the dead in order to be free of them. Introducing the ethics of the new theater, he declares that despite the processes of nature there is still the human choice. Real persons do not like actors vanish when their parts are done. In sum, man is haunted.

No, replies the Player King, there is no such permanence in being and no such particularity in human relations.

> PLAYER KING: This world is not for aye, nor 'tis not strange

> That even our loves should with our for-
> tunes change.

The Player Queen, argues the King, imagines that her actions in the future will express her present feelings. But the
part one plays is determined by events, not by oneself.
Man is subject to laws. In a disjunctive sequence of platitudes, the King establishes that passions founder in the alteration of circumstances. The plot, not the actor, decides
the action.

> Our wills and fates do so contrary run
> That our devices still are overthrown.

What seems a fixed resolve is but a sentiment clinging to
some past state of affairs:

> Purpose is but the slave to memory,
> Of violent birth but poor validity:
> Which now like fruit unripe sticks on the tree.

If the Player Queen persists in her loyalty, her action will
be a compulsive attachment to the past, like Hamlet's to
his dead father. To be true actors we must eliminate from
ourselves such untimely leftovers of feeling. We need
oblivion behind us.

> Most necessary 'tis that we forget
> To pay ourselves what to ourselves is debt.

Our situation is as we find it, and we ought to match our
moods to its demands. With her husband alive, let the
Player Queen believe that she will be eternally faithful to
him. But let her recognize too that her feeling is but a reflection of the present moment and will vanish when things
change.

So think thou wilt no second husband wed;
But die thy thoughts when thy first lord is dead.

In *The Mouse-trap* the individual is nothing else than the situation in which he is acting. To the extent that he engages himself in it, he exists; in evading it through "What to ourselves in passion we propose," he fails in his part and becomes nobody. In *The Mouse-trap,* the impersonal values of the traditional theater and its communal background are criticized from the viewpoint of modern individualism: "the story is extant."

Wrote John Dewey, to whom the error of Western philosophy lay in perpetuating the Greek concept of being: "Think of any human adult in a concrete way, and at once you must place him in some 'social' context and functional relationship—parent, citizen, employer, wage-earner, farmer, merchant, teacher, lawyer, good citizen, criminal —and so on indefinitely." * Man is a role player, and dies, or should be considered dead, when his "operant powers their functions leave to do." On the stage of *The Mouse-trap*—which is the old world come to life again, but with its heroic poetry replaced by doggerel, absurd metaphors and bad rhetoric—one is real insofar as one has a part in a set of visible relations. There is no individual until there is an actor, no concrete existence except in the "functional relationships." The play's the thing.

The philosophy of the Player King thus becomes a justification of Gertrude's remarriage, ironically presented by Hamlet to expose the mechanism of thought responsible for her betrayal of his father. The nature of existence itself, when seen as bounded by the visible stage, demanded that she replace her dead husband—and as quickly as possible.

* *Liberalism and Social Actions,* John Dewey, G. P. Putnam, publisher, 1935.

The interchangeability of individuals is an ethical principle of life conceived as function. A magistrate in a totalitarian country was quoted some years ago as being shocked by the insistence of some women on remaining attached to husbands condemned to labor camps. The proper rule, he declared, was that "when the husband is arrested, the wife sues for divorce and looks for another man." To keep the "social context" intact as a source of roles for others, parts that have ceased to function ought to be replaced. The death of her husband threatens to deprive the Player Queen of her role. But an unengaged actress lacks "concreteness." Therefore, the choices available to the Player Queen are: to acquire another husband; go offstage into oblivion (solitude, suicide); or accept a new part, that of the widow. Going offstage would be the worst choice. As between the other two: why prefer a new part to one she is already skilled in playing? Why one set of functional relationships rather than another? In choosing her new part in advance of the event—

> Both here and hence, pursue me lasting strife,
> If once a widow, ever I be wife!—

the Player Queen has committed herself as recklessly as Hamlet did in his peevish opposition to the universal fate of fathers.

The Mouse-trap principle of substitution is also a justification for Fortinbras who, when the war against Denmark was called off, marched his "list of lawless resolutes" against the Poles. Shall a man renounce the enterprise upon which his dramatic existence depends because his enemy has failed him? Shall the political actor watch his concreteness dwindle when through acquiring a new foe he can restore himself to his "social context and functional relationship"?

Besides attacking his enemies, *The Mouse-trap* reflects Hamlet's own lust for action and the bad dreams that arise from his self-restraint until the particular "What I have to do" reveals itself. Ceaseless activity is the categorical imperative of the stage within the stage. On the large stage, the living vacillate and draw back; the ebb and flow of their feelings does not correspond to the fixity of their relations as mothers, fathers, husbands, sons; the metamorphosis of their relations does not correspond to the fixity of their feelings as criminals, lovers, avengers. For the living the time is out of joint, and the act of true color can come only in a moment of providential concurrence of vision and opportunity.

With Hamlet the gap between the individual and his visible situation results in the tension of the double action of performing on the stage while pressing toward the invisible event. This tension expresses itself in exposures and self-critical soliloquies as the hero's consciousness keeps prying at the hidden dimensions of his situation. The overall mood is the bitterness of suspended action in the interval before the gap can be bridged. In *The Mouse-trap,* that "knavish piece of work," the gap is closed through choosing among the parts and proclaiming the death of the past.

On the large stage there is the reality that passes show and the possibility of the deed of true color. In *The Mouse-trap* there is the reality of being in the trap and the necessity of accommodating oneself to that reality. On the large stage, art and fact are in opposition to each other, and life consists of experiencing that opposition. Hamlet cannot formulate the "matter" that is particular to him except in action and language that partly hide it behind the seeming of accepted forms. The closer he comes to the invisible event, the more it must appear

That not your trespass, but my madness speaks.

In *The Mouse-trap* art and fact are one. Living is structural, and only the structural can be lived.

Apart from the result he anticipates from its performance, Hamlet is tempted by *The Mouse-trap* as a solution for his tormenting situation. If he could make himself over according to the model of the players, he too could forget "to pay himself" and still be rid of the self-accusation of bestial oblivion. By putting on the players' play he has demonstrated that he knows how dramatic fictions are produced.

Would not this, sir . . . if the rest of my fortunes turn Turk with me . . . get me a fellowship in a cry of players, sir?

If completely defeated, he can, as a last resort, turn himself into an actor.

VIII

No cue has come for the longed-for act and Hamlet's will is inadequate to initiate it. As the ghost left the platform at Elsinore, however, another movement had begun in Hamlet, a movement to purge himself of every experience unrelated to the hidden plot.

HAMLET: Yea, from the table of my memory
I'll wipe away all trivial fond recòrds,
All saws of books, all forms, all pressures past,
That youth and observation copied there;
And thy commandment all alone shall live
Within the book and volume of my brain,
Unmix'd with baser matter: yes, yes, by heaven!

In this mood of self-purification he has bidden an anguished farewell to Ophelia. Unable to begin his action, he has begun to make himself over for the act to come, a kind of pre-initiation ritual. Claudius notes uneasily that unexplained changes are afoot:

> Something have you heard
> Of Hamlet's transformation; so I call it,
> Since not th' exterior nor the inward man
> Resembles what it was: what it should be,
> More than his father's death, that thus hath put him
> So much from th' understanding of himself,
> I cannot dream of.

Hamlet's negative movement of self-transformation parallels the experience of religious conversion. It takes place, however, on the stage which is the world, not on the Other Stage of spirit. The place where an inner action takes place is decisive—it is by its dramatic location that the self-discipline of a tightrope artist differs from that of a saint. Hamlet's movement is toward action by way of changing the actor, not toward a detached spiritual condition.

Historically, Hamlet's inner conflict reflects the stalemate reached in modern times between the individual as public, or community, figure and the individual as a being conscious of his own uniqueness. Hamlet's self-negating dedication to the "commandment" of the ghost asserts that this stalemate is intolerable, and that, feeling himself falsified by his performance, the individual is impelled to erase the "trivial fond recòrds" on which his identity is founded and to launch himself into the unknown. Thus Hamlet's half-jesting "good" in response to Claudius's death plans for him is also an earnest assent and a prophecy. In the voyage to England he foresees the culmination of his effort to join hands with the dead and to resolve the tragedy of his father's death. His last words before his departure predict his transformation into the Avenger:

> O, from this time forth,
> My thoughts be bloody, or be nothing worth.

Death and renewal come to Hamlet in his crossing of the water. His rebirth alters the tempo of the play. The heightening of his crisis, unexplained by any overt episode, begins at night on shipboard—"in my heart there was a kind of fighting that would not let me sleep." He has become totally imprisoned by his helplessness: "I lay worse than the mutines in the bilboes." And then, inspired to purloin from his sleeping companions the death warrant issued for him by Claudius, he feels the invisible event take hold and lead him directly to his revenge.

> HAMLET: Being thus be-netted round with villainies,—
> Ere I could make a prologue to my brains
> They had begun the play . . .

In describing to Horatio what had happened on shipboard, Hamlet makes it clear that his stalemate had become absolute and that it was broken by the rise to the surface of the hidden drama: ". . . when our deep plots do pall . . . There's a divinity that shapes our ends."

Upon his return to Denmark, Hamlet is no longer the man-actor trying in vain to discover his part. *His* plot has palled. Now, like the ghost itself, he is an actor who has returned from offstage. "High and mighty," he writes to Claudius in the symbolism of rebirth, "You shall know I am set naked on your kingdom." His first appearance is in the churchyard, as if he had risen from one of the graves there, or were a corpse turned up by the gravediggers. "Has this fellow no feeling of his business?" he jests as he comes on. The clown is there to bury people, not to unbury them by opening the floor of the stage.

In this conversation on death that follows, Hamlet puts flesh back on the skeletons, like one who had seen them alive. "That skull had a tongue in it, and could sing once," and so on. Of being dead he says, "Here's fine revolution, an we had the trick to see't! [He has just been through that revolution.] Did these bones cost no more the breeding, but to play at loggats with 'em? *Mine ache to think on't.*"

When did the clown become a gravedigger? "Every fool can tell that," says he. "It was the very day that young Hamlet was born." (Critics point out that this speech contains an error of calculation: if the physical birth of Hamlet were meant, Shakespeare would be contradicting other statements regarding Hamlet's age. But every fool can tell that Hamlet has been born twice.)

Leaping into the grave of Ophelia the new Hamlet announces himself. His identity is no longer in question and he no longer hesitates about his feelings or his capacity for action. In quick succession he challenges Laertes, declares his passion for the dead Ophelia ("Why, I will fight with him upon this theme . . . I lov'd Ophelia"), and assures Horatio that he has the "perfect conscience to quit him [Claudius] with his arm." The time of collision for which he has been yearning ("O, 'tis most sweet, When in one line two crafts directly meet") has come. The single act for which he lives is about to be performed. The time allowed (that is, before the King learns what happened to his messengers)

> . . . will be short; the interim is mine;
> And a man's life's no more than to say 'one.'

So the newly unified Hamlet will kill Claudius. His action will not, however, solve the dilemma of the man-actor. Hamlet can now say, "I am constant to my purposes"; but he must contradict himself by adding, "they follow the King's pleasure." The situation has been completely clarified, and he is no longer struggling for the is against the seems. Now "the readiness is all"; all the gaps are closed, and he is being moved at last. He is certain that the thing he has to do will be accomplished, and through him. Yet it will not be his act, but the part prepared for him before he entered the stage. The plot has won against the man, which is to say that the past has triumphed over the present, the dead over the living. Hamlet has become the weapon of his father against Claudius. The hero fulfills the necessity inherent in past actions; through this fulfillment he makes way for the new. But he can accomplish his end only in renouncing himself.

The triumph of the plot over the hero ("there's a special providence in the fall of a sparrow") is exposed in the accidental character of Hamlet's revenge in the course of the "foolery" of the fencing match. His sudden turning on Claudius lacks the true color for which he had been striving. But his ambiguous "Follow my mother!" as the King dies sets this accidental finish in another perspective, that of the story turned into an ageless pageant of Claudius pursuing Gertrude, with his murdered brother ahead of her and the avenging son at his heels.

In becoming equal to the plot Hamlet experiences the nostalgia of the transcending hero for human accident and self-contradiction. Upon his return from England his misery is no longer that of violent vacillation between is and seems, expressing itself in tortured monologues and angry wit. His mockery of Osric is in his old style, but it has a

tone of detachment and farewell—"the bubbles are out"—
and there are no more soliloquies. The anguish of the re-
born Hamlet is accompanied by a sad feeling of inevitability:

But thou wouldst not think how ill all's here about my heart;
but it is no matter . . . If it be now, 'tis not to come; if it be
not to come, it will be now; if it be not now, yet it will come:
the readiness is all.

The descent into death has taught Hamlet the resigned
"yet it will come" to events, as the alternative to the "I'll
do it pat" of the conscious will.

The dilemma of the man-actor remains. On the stage
which is the world the plot is written by nobody and no
one can denote himself truly. In the end the dying Hamlet
cries to the audience of "this chance" that his mystery is
still unrevealed: "Had I but time . . . O, I could tell you
—But let it be." His story cannot be told (of course, it has
been told), perhaps because he was alone in it with the
dead, while even Oedipus had Jocasta as a fellow sufferer.
It is left for Horatio to "speak . . . How these things
came about" without a mind to give shape to them. It is the
image of human history,

> Of carnal, bloody, and unnatural acts;
> Of accidental judgements, casual slaughters;
> Of deaths put on by cunning and forc'd cause . . .

The drama in which the living man attempted in vain to
seize his life as particular to him concludes by proclaiming
the utter irony of human existence as Fortinbras orders a
soldier's burial for Hamlet, not for what he did but for
what he might have done—

> For he was likely, had he been put on,
> To have prov'd most royally.

Military pomp befits this emissary of the dead who, having demonstrated the impotence of him who knows not seems, became the soldier of a forced cause and succeeded finally in littering the stage with corpses, in "Such a sight as . . . Becomes the field, but here shews much amiss." Life has mixed itself inseparably into art.

5

A Psychological Case

The peculiarity of *The Idiot* is that its hero is almost a spectator. "I've really come to meet people," explains Myshkin on his arrival from Switzerland. From his first encounter with Rogozhin on the train, he has, however, stepped into a complex underground intrigue involving Nastasya Filipovna, Ganya, the Yepanchin family, the Ivolgins, Lebedev, Totsky, and, of course, Rogozhin himself. Unhesitatingly, Myshkin allows himself to be drawn into it, but without altering his onlooker's attitude. By the end of Part I, on the very day of his return to Russia, he has offered to marry Nastasya, become the "rival" of Rogozhin, aroused the interest of Aglaya and the impatience of Ganya, and received confidences from several quarters. Wrote Dostoyevsky in his *The Notebooks to the Idiot,* underscoring the entry, *"The chief thing is that they all need him"*—among other things, as their audience. He is the understanding listener, always available. Thus he attracts to himself all the personages of the narrative in a perpetual round of comings and goings, confessions and revelations, in pace not unlike bedroom farce.

Throughout the novel, Myshkin plays opposite a cast of garrulous types who amble about in episodes instigated by self-delusion, greed, ambition, conventionality, desperation, and sheer love of absurdity and troublemaking. The reader is dipped into twenty years of Russian debate on such topics as the Russian character, capital punishment, religion, materialism, individual charity, the future of the aristocracy. Beyond everything else, however, Dostoyevsky is a virtuoso of dramatic stagecraft, able to pull out of his hat an endless string of surprises. No sooner does a situation begin to coalesce than it is blown apart again by a new revelation, an unexpected arrival. Dostoyevsky's playings with Lebedev's purloined wallet and with the "case of Pavlishchev's son" are peaks of inventiveness in keeping the reader off balance; they match on the plane of comedy the build-up of tensions in the great, passionate confrontations, such as Nastasya's unexpected visit to the home of Ganya and her showdown with Aglaya.

Myshkin's part in both the vaudevilles and the climaxes is that of a sympathetic bystander ready to lend a hand; even when the action is aimed at him he commiserates with those who are trying to cheat him or to use him to settle emotional accounts. Through his self-abnegation, he is an impersonal witness during his most earnest participation. For all his readiness to enter into everyone's life, he is and remains an outsider, an "idiot" in the classical meaning of a private or unrelated person. "He's as much of a stranger to me as to anyone else," exclaims Aglaya, his "fiancée," after Myshkin has spoiled their betrothal party by throwing a fit. Instead of being engaged in the action of the novel, the Prince blesses it by his presence. He hovers above the fatal pursuit of Nastasya by Rogozhin like an angel wringing his hands over the Crucifixion. In the end, his embrace of the murderer by the bedside of the immolated bride transforms the killing into a ritual sacrifice.

Myshkin's detached character is, as Dostoyevsky observes in *The Notebooks,* the *idea* of *The Idiot.* In him the reader was to see "how Russia is reflected." We know that it was Myshkin's sudden coming to life in Dostoyevsky's imagination that enabled him to start writing the work after half a dozen drafts centered upon an "idiot" with a different (highly active) character had proved sterile. Dostoyevsky, too, "needed" Myshkin to bless his undertaking. Like Hamlet's, the personality of the Prince overflows the plot, a Dostoyevskian recasting of the familiar romantic tragedy of a rich young man and a woman of blemished reputation. Myshkin is not shaped by the action; it is, rather, a background against which his uniqueness is revealed. For all its intensity, the love triangle, like the subsidiary intrigues spun through the narrative, is but an occasion for Myshkin to practice his irreducible talent for giving himself. "So as to make the Idiot's character more fascinating (more charming)," Dostoyevsky wrote, "he has to be imagined in a field of action."

The notion of a *field* of action is an interesting alternative to the traditional idea of a plot as a *structure* of actions. Instead of seeking to define its hero by the continuity of his deeds, *The Idiot* spreads outward to envelop as many aspects of his personality as possible. The "field" is made up of a mosaic of episodes that do not move toward a resolution or even bear any necessary relation to one another. Stressing multiplicity rather than coherence, Dostoyevsky advised himself to "prepare many incidents and stories." The affair of Rogozhin and Nastasya is but one of the situations through which the Prince's character comes to light; other sides of him are shown in his idyllic meeting with Aglaya in the park, his relations with Kolya, his responses to the machinations of Lebedev and the Burdovsky crowd and to the "protest" of Ippolit.

At bottom, Myshkin's feelings are directed past the framework of *The Idiot* toward events in Russia and the Russian folk. "In his most *tragic,* most *personal* moments," declares *The Notebooks,* "the Prince is concerned with solving general problems. . . . When *at the end of the 4th part* N.F. again deserts the Prince and runs away with Rogozhin on her wedding day, the Prince is wholly absorbed with the club [of the children]." I know of no other instance of a novelist planning to have his hero turn his back on the novel's greatest scenes. The detachment of Myshkin contemplated by this note would make Camus's Stranger seem like a passionate lover. In the completed work, Myshkin does not, of course, attain this degree of absence. Yet it is significant that Dostoyevsky thought him capable of it, and it is a fact that, as Dostoyevsky also notes, "the Prince has had only *the slightest effect* on the protagonists' lives." (All italics are Dostoyevsky's.)

Myshkin's function is not to alter the course of the action but to disseminate the aura of a new state of being, let events occur as they will. *The Idiot* is Dostoyevsky's book of salvation, but Christ, too, saved without overcoming the implacability of destiny. As the personification of the highest potentialities of the Russian spirit, the Prince illuminates (or "reflects") the Russian predicament in lightning flashes of grace. From abroad, Dostoyevsky surveys the deepening chaos and depravity of Russian society, and to his unhappy country he dispatches Myshkin as the redeemer—an equivalent of his hope that *The Idiot* will redeem him from his creditors and allow him to return home. The mood of the novel is troubled; it occurs to Dostoyevsky that in its large cast of characters "everyone is a traitor." Still, the author's nostalgia for the motherland and for Russians, even at their worst, comes through in the vivacity and good humor of his characterizations. Russia as represented in *The Idiot* is peopled by types in which the corruptions of the European—lack of faith, vanity, boredom, fatuousness, lechery, lust for money—are heightened. Its Saint Petersburg setting had long been for Dostoyevsky a dreamlike frontier where the grand wraiths of Western literature and history—the Iagos, Micawbers, Rastignacs, Richelieus, Napoleons, Marie Antoinettes, Camilles— mingled with the creatures of Gogol and Pushkin. In the capital there now also appeared new types, born out of the materialistic ideologies of Europe—types out of whose midst Raskolnikov had sprung and who are represented in *The Idiot* by the group that accompanies Pavlishchev's son, characterized by Dostoyevsky in a letter to the writer Maikov as "some types of the modern Positivist among the highly 'extreme' young men."

These alien presences are everywhere; the behavior of Russia's aristocratic, commercial and intellectual classes is regulated by them. What makes matters especially desperate is Russian naïveté—the native genius for belief and enthusiasm, which causes Russians to carry out in action what the West with its coldness and caution is content to confine to art or abstract thought. "If one of us becomes a Catholic," cries Myshkin in his tirade at the Yepanchin party, "he is bound to become a Jesuit, and one of the most subterranean. If one of us becomes an atheist, he is bound to demand the uprooting of faith in God by force, that is, of course, by the sword. . . . And our people do not simply become atheists, they infallibly *believe* in atheism."

Rogozhin, Nastasya has told him, "drives everything to a point where it grows into a passion." He is thus a true Russian, a forerunner of Mitya Karamazov, and though Dostoyevsky sees his hunger for Nastasya as equivalent to his father's lust for gold pieces, he respects Rogozhin for the wholeness of his passion. Dostoyevsky's conviction of the susceptibility of the Russians *vis-à-vis* their European models (he himself borrowed prolifically from French and British authors) gives his fiction its political edge, while his identification with Russian extremism as both a dangerous weakness and a sacred gift is the basis of his emotional nationalism. "Everywhere and in everything," he wrote to Maikov, "I go to the ultimate limit; all my life I have crossed beyond the frontier."

Dostoyevsky's hopes for Myshkin as a saving power rest on his theory of emulation, which conceives of dramatic fictions as constituting the roots of human action. In the opening pages of Part IV, which the author jokingly compares to "some critical review in a periodical," he presents the view that actual people are merely "watered-down" types out of novels and plays. Average persons are creatures of fiction reproduced in countless rough copies. Aware of their commonplaceness, "they simply refuse to be what they are and do their utmost to be original and independent without possessing the qualities of independence." In sum, men prefer to imitate models rather than seek their own reality. Social life is thus dominated by inventions of the imagination, by personages who are "perhaps an exaggeration but not by any means a myth.'" Without fictional heroes, nothing of significance takes place; after the death of Nastasya and the elimination of Myshkin and Rogozhin, all that is left to say is that "Lebedev, Keller, Ganya, Ptitsyn, and the many other characters of our story are carrying on as before, have changed little, and we have almost nothing to tell about them." Life not only copies art but derives from art its reason for being lived.

In *The Idiot,* the supreme example of mediocrity is Ganya, whom Dostoyevsky detests for his smug and self-deceptive pretensions to distinction. Ganya enters the narrative as if he were made up for the stage, and everything about him is artifice. "He was a very good-looking young man. . . . Only his smile, for all its amiability, was somewhat too exquisite, revealing a row of altogether too dazzling and even teeth." Confronted by Ganya's smile, the Prince, despite his charitable attitude, suspects that "when he is alone he doesn't look like that at all and, quite possibly, he never laughs." Whatever Ganya does is destined to be counterfeit. When Nastasya throws Rogozhin's rubles into the fireplace and offers them to Ganya if he will pull them out, Ganya, "in his evening clothes, his gloves and his hat in his hand, with his arms folded," adopts a noble stance and refuses to budge. His striving for dignity is more than he can endure, and as he watches the flames leap around the wrapping of the rubles "an insane smile wandered over his chalk-white face," and he suddenly falls forward unconscious. The fainting of Ganya, brought on by his inner conflict, is an imitation of the fit that seizes Myshkin when he tries to behave with dignity at the Yepanchin party in order to please Aglaya. Ganya's heroics gain him nothing. "He didn't pull it out, he held firm!" exclaims Nastasya in momentary admiration, then adds, "Which means that his vanity is even greater than his lust for money." Whatever course Ganya chooses, mediocrity remains his typical characteristic.

But though commonplace people are incapable of originating anything, they cannot be overlooked, Dostoyevsky insists, "for ordinary people are nearly always the link in the chain of human affairs." History is the conflict of types, each the personification of a passion and a fixed idea that drags in its wake hordes of self-deluded imitators. "Some of our young women had only to cut their hair short, put on blue spectacles, and call themselves Nihilists, to persuade themselves at once that, having put on their spectacles, they have immediately acquired 'convictions' of their own." It is by equating the idea with the costume (the blue spectacles) that the masses of mimics become "links" between ideas and their realization. The Napoleonic idea gives rise to the image of Raskolnikov, upon the publication of whose story an actual student named Danilov promptly murders a pawnbroker out of "principle." *Crime and Punishment* is concerned with the privileges of the history-making archetypes as against the mere "links." In *The Idiot,* Dostoyevsky undertakes to employ for his own ends the processes by which the fictional types dominate human existence.

It is his grasp of the dynamics of these quasi-fictional beings, both unique and ordinary, as they appear in the streets and drawing rooms of Saint Petersburg that constitutes Dostoyevsky's "realism." Dostoyevsky denies that he is a "psychologist," but he claims deep insight into the states of the soul of typical characters. "I have my own idea about art," he wrote to the critic Strachov shortly after finishing *The Idiot,* "and it is this: What most people regard as fantastic and lacking in universality, *I* hold to be the inmost essence of truth. Arid observation of everyday trivialities I have long since ceased to regard as realism. . . . Is not my fantastic 'Idiot' the very dailiest truth? Precisely such characters *must* exist in those strata of our society which have divorced themselves from the soil—which are actually becoming fantastic."

Inhabited by dream personages—the Rogozhins, Nastasyas, Yepanchins, Princesses Belokonsky, Totskys, Lebedevs, Burdovskys, Ivolgins—Russia is plunging toward anarchy. Reason cannot avert the catastrophe, since reason itself only produces fantastic types of its own—the Positivists and Nihilists of the radical younger generation, with their "logical" assumptions and their disregard of human feelings. The only chance for salvation is the appearance of a type of a different order—the embodiment of what to Dostoyevsky was "the Russian idea." In conceiving Myshkin as "the wholly beautiful man," the messiah of love and brotherhood alive in the depths of Russian piety, and manifesting himself under the conditions of contemporary Russian life, Dostoyevsky sought to demonstrate that Russian literature could take control of Russian history, and through it of world history ("the renaissance of the whole of mankind and its resurrection by Russian thought"), by means of an original figure personifying the deepest national feelings undistorted by Western rationalism. The "idiocy" of *The Idiot* is a declaration of independence from alien philosophies and literary models, good or bad. The outstanding virtue of Myshkin is that he is "ours." "Any Russian who says, writes, or does something of his own, something that is his *by right* and not borrowed, inevitably becomes national, though he may not be able to speak Russian correctly. I regard this as an axiom." As the creator of a new Russian type, Dostoyevsky did not hesitate to regard himself as a shaper of the future.

The messianic content of *The Idiot* is in conflict with the dramatic form of Dostoyevsky's major novels. If the role of the tragic hero is to heighten the action and drive it toward its dénouement, the mission of Myshkin is the reverse—to soften passions and to arrest the dramatic conflict or to divert it. He hopes to "rehabilitate" Nastasya by convincing her of her innocence, and to awaken compassion in the obsessed Rogozhin. He endeavors to sweeten the rancor of the "son of Pavlishchev" and his rowdy crew, to soothe Aglaya's hurt *amour-propre,* to heal the break between Lebedev and General Ivolgin. Myshkin is less a dramatic figure than an edifying one. He offers an example of liberation from the centrifugal pull of self and of actions once they are under way. Nor was the continuing openness of Dostoyevsky's "Prince Christ" intended to affect only the characters of *The Idiot;* as I have suggested, it was to extend to the readers of the novel as well. With Myshkin, the art of fiction is redirected to serve an interest of the mind more urgent than art: the search for what man can be. This is the political substance of the novel—a politics that is inherently metaphysical. With his character reflected on many planes of experience, the Prince projects out of *The Idiot* as a personage who could manifest himself in situations of actual life. Myshkin has brought into being the "Myshkin type," as an earlier relaxation, or opening out, of the contours of drama brought into being the "Hamlet personality." Fulfilling the design of his author, Myshkin has passed from literature into social history. He is a rival of those potent fictions—the Dandy, Superman, the Proletariat—that the imagination of the nineteenth century provided as models for men reaching for new possibilities of conduct. He, too, is a "spectre haunting Europe." He is the original of those who seek to persuade through self-renunciation, from the lover who "understands" his mistress's infidelities to flower children of the 1960's convinced of the perfidiousness of the adult mind. Composed a hundred years ago, *The Idiot* is an advanced instance of the modernist mingling of art and life. It is a work that is itself an action aimed at producing social, cultural, and even political consequences. No doubt Dostoyevsky had in mind both the art of the novel and this potential force of *The Idiot* when he summed up his judgment of the work by saying that "there's much in the novel . . . that didn't come off, but something did come off. I don't stand behind my novel, but I do stand behind my idea."

Afloat between history and fiction, and only marginally related to the events of *The Idiot*, Myshkin is like a divine messenger in Homer or the Old Testament, and also a figure who seems about to turn into the abstract person of a religious or political tract. Dostoyevsky was acutely aware that to make Myshkin credible he had to prevent him from becoming the bearer of a philosophy, and he kept reminding himself to bring forth his hero's meaning through behavior, not through words. "N.B.: The Prince is like a Sphinx," he enters in his *Notebooks*. "He reveals himself without any explanations on the author's part, except perhaps in the first chapter." In this difficult effort to deliver his "idea" in the form of a living personality, Dostoyevsky is remarkably successful; the Prince is an outstanding demonstration that Dostoyevsky's "types" have a dynamic reality different from those in other fiction. On occasion, Myshkin does fall into sermonizing ("You are a philosopher and you've come to teach us," remarks Adelaida, signaling Dostoyevsky's awareness that his hero has slipped into lecturing), and several of his speeches, notably the one preceding his fit at the Yepanchins', are in their aggressive class consciousness out of character and unashamedly proclaim the political philosophy of his author. Yet so firmly has Myshkin been imagined that his very lapses confirm our recognition of him as an individual.

The vividness of Myshkin thrusts the central drama of *The Idiot* into the background. The romance of Rogozhin and Nastasya, in which the Prince has intervened, is realized in three great scenes, or "acts," that possess the unity of tragedy: the grand finale of Part II, in which Nastasya rushes off with Rogozhin and is pursued by the Prince; the mysterious confrontation of Myshkin and Rogozhin and the latter's attempt to murder the Prince in the dark hallway; and the concluding scene of the novel, in which the murdered Nastasya is joined by her two "lovers." To focus the novel on these coherently related scenes tremendously heightens its poetic effect. But the poetry thus achieved belongs, for all the innovating chiaroscuro of the love intrigue, to the order of romantic drama, and it is gained at the expense of the new pathos represented by the figure of Myshkin and the state of the other principal characters.

There is a tragic drama within *The Idiot,* but, like *Hamlet,* it is a set piece out of a more conventional literature. To read *The Idiot* as a tragedy or a "tragic novel" requires cutting across the vast disorder of episodes (from Myshkin's conversation with the Yepanchin butler to General Ivolgin's affair with the captain's widow) and the activities of subordinate and late-appearing characters—such as Ippolit—that constitute the real body of the novel and the "field of action" that supplies Myshkin's magnetism. The bitter affair of Rogozhin and Nastasya comes to the surface of the narrative on a few tense occasions, but it has a way of sinking out of sight the moment the Prince is withdrawn from it; there is not a single scene in which the lovers are together without him. In substance and structure, *The Idiot* is closer to grand opera or to a chronicle containing ceremonial scenes than to tragedy. The pursuit of the self-doomed beauty by her single-minded victim-destroyer is a colorful leitmotif threaded through the scheming, drinking, lechery, gossip, and matchmaking carried on as on a stage set of a village fair by a chorus of posturing society folk, matrons, marriageable daughters, eligible young men, mistresses, beggars, landladies, roughnecks, students, and clowns.

The ineffable closing scene, in which Rogozhin and Myshkin lie in each other's arms at the foot of the altarlike bed bearing the corpse of their slaughtered darling, is a tableau composed of effigies that could be carried on a float in a procession; the editor of *The Notebooks* describes it as a "lyrical and deathly still-life." The motionless vision becomes the emblem of Myshkin's transcendent power—a kind of inverted heavenly kingdom of love, madness, and death where the emotionally disengaged Prince attains final communion with the lovers purged of self.

That *The Idiot* is the most "musical" of Dostoyevsky's novels is related to the looseness of its action. Instead of pivoting on a single deed, as in *Crime and Punishment* or *The Brothers Karamazov,* the narrative rises and falls in tides of feeling keyed to the illuminated state of the Prince. The poles of Myshkin's "idiocy" are the black despair and magical released moments of the conversion experience. In Switzerland, he was sunk in depression until his senses were awakened by the sudden bray of a donkey; then his feeling of being lost in a foreign place vanished and he "liked the whole of Switzerland." The Prince has looked at life through the eyes of the condemned prisoner facing his last minutes on earth. His uplifted condition is reaffirmed by his response to Adelaida when she asks him to tell about being in love. "I have not been in love," the Prince replies. "I . . . was happy in a different way."

But Myshkin is not the only transformed person in *The Idiot.* All its leading characters have passed over into conditions that estrange them from their former selves, though on different psychic levels. Nastasya is breaking with her past with Totsky and is casting herself adrift. Rogozhin, like Myshkin a recent invalid, and still running a fever, feels released by the death of his father and has set out on his hunt for love. Ippolit, the dying youth facing his brick wall, has, like the prisoner on the scaffold described by Myshkin, heard the hymn to life in the blackness of being deprived of it. Aglaya keeps changing before Myshkin's eyes from a "child woman" to a "woman child." Even secondary figures, such as Ganya and Lebedev, seem to alter their characters—at times as if by an afterthought of the author. A book of salvation, *The Idiot* is also a book of conversions; that is, of persons whose salvation is at issue. All are engaged in trying out in action the implications of a new position. Everyone is at the edge of an end and a beginning, whether through inheriting a fortune, getting married, or committing suicide. We find in *The Notebooks,* "the Prince and his activity: Aglaya *convertie.* Rogozhin cuts N.F.'s throat."

The characters are in a state of "enthusiasm" and gifted with clairvoyance. After scrutinizing the photograph of Nastasya, the Prince declares that he can "read faces," and throughout the novel he arouses surprise by identifying the feeling hidden behind the social performance. He is a kind of investigating agent, a divine counterpart of the investigating magistrate Porfiry in *Crime and Punishment.* "Kolya and the Prince as spies," says an odd item in *The Notebooks.* Other characters, too, see into each other and reveal what they see with an absence of inhibition that often breaks out into a scandal. Aglaya understands Ganya's calculations, and Nastasya is aware of every nuance of his motives. Rogozhin, too, is transparent to Nastasya, though she is incapable of making use of this knowledge. A wounding candor is achieved, which Myshkin is inclined to salute as the shock of newly attained innocence. His own charm consists primarily in acknowledging things to be as they are, undistorted by vanity or self-seeking. Everyone deceives him, but in encountering recognition of their tentative identities, instead of resistance, all are compelled to confront themselves. It is this that causes Ippolit to hate Myshkin and Nastasya to run away from him.

Surrounded by indeterminate persons, semi-fictions striving to locate themselves in existence, Myshkin, the hero of light and quiet who was "happy in a different way," yearns during recurring intervals of pressure to retreat from the world of adults to his peaceful kingdom of children and donkeys. In the perspective established by his presence, the action, though musical and full of color, is the sound and fury of people driven beyond themselves into abstract roles. "I'll go on the streets," Nastasya keeps proclaiming. "Or I'll be a washerwoman." In *The Idiot*, the validity of action is questioned not philosophically, as in *Hamlet*, but in terms of its psychological reality. Herein lie the modernity of the novel and its continuing relevance. The styles of action prevailing in Russia and the West are subjected to scrutiny and prove to contain a core of mental aberration. "It's a psychological case, not an action," observes Totsky, after Ferdyshenko has recounted the "worst action" of his life. A similar judgment haunts every action of the novel. Between the actor and his act falls the shadow of pathology. Is not Rogozhin's tracking down of Nastasya also a "case" and not an action? Telling Myshkin of the beginning of his love affair, Rogozhin implies that his passion is an obsession originating in his desire to destroy himself in order to escape his father's wrath. "And actually, before I went there [to Nastasya's] I never thought of coming back alive anyway." Nastasya's "scenes" constantly raise the issue of her sanity. When Rogozhin bursts into her party with his hundred thousand rubles, General Yepanchin anxiously asks Totsky, who knows her best, whether "she hasn't gone off her head. . . . I don't mean it metaphorically but in a strictly medical sense." Myshkin is convinced that she is demented and confesses to Radomsky, near the end of the novel, that he has been frightened of her from first sight. The narrator himself, reviewing the persons of his tale, refers to Rogozhin and Nastasya as a madman and a madwoman. The sickness of Myshkin is writ large in the title of the novel. He describes himself as an invalid who cannot marry, and his refusal to condemn violence and falsehood is as consistent with the attitude of a mental patient toward fellow inmates as with Christian forgiveness. In *The Notebooks,* Myshkin's blending of saintliness and diagnostic concern is made explicit. "The Prince says of sinful persons: All sick people have to be taken care of."

Thus, though *The Idiot,* with its constant dramatic explosions, is one of the most animated novels in literature, action in it is vitiated by the ambiguous condition of the actors, expressed in fantasizing on different levels—from Ippolit's nightmares to General Ivolgin's "memories." The motives of the characters tend to realize themselves in reverse. Rogozhin exchanges crosses with Myshkin, asks his mother to bless Myshkin, then tries to cut his throat. Nastasya, in love with Myshkin and frantic to escape Rogozhin, tries to induce Aglaya to marry Myshkin and promises to marry Rogozhin when this has been accomplished. The Dostoyevskian character cannot trust his feelings or decisions; some aberrant impulse may cause him to act contrary to them. At their height, the conflicts of the characters reach an intensity beyond rhetorical formulation and hurtle into the physiological, as when Myshkin responds to Rogozhin's lifted knife by falling in a fit, or in the instance of Ganya's faint. The inability of the actors to sustain their identities in the face of the action dissipates their tragic pathos, as if Othello were struck down by a heart attack after smothering Desdemona. Instead of pity and fear, the slaying of Nastasya inspires musical reverberations throughout the consciousness; the reader experiences not a resolution of the events but the feeling of being on the verge of a revelation.

In *The Idiot,* the *Hamlet* pathos reappears; it arises not from the terribleness of the action, as in tragedy, but from the characters' desperate longing to act. This longing is dramatized by the consumptive Ippolit when, with but a few weeks to live, he decides to end his life by a public gesture, in order, he declares, "to take advantage of the last possibility of *action*" (Dostoyevsky's italics). The sole reason for Ippolit's presence in the novel is to bring up this issue of action in the face of its cancellation by sickness; to achieve authenticity, Ippolit's act must eliminate the actor —that is, himself. Planning the part of Ippolit, Dostoyevsky designates him in *The Notebooks* as "the main axis of the whole novel" and instructs himself to "center the whole plot on him." Like many other notions in *The Notebooks,* this scheme for Ippolit is not carried out in the finished work. He is not the "axis" of the story; after his moment in the spotlight, the plot passes him by and he all but drops out of sight. In respect to the action he is not a major figure but, rather, a leftover from the *Idiot* of the early drafts—one of the "insulted and injured," who villainously avenges himself upon life, a male adolescent Nastasya. If Dostoyevsky is able to think of him as an alternative hero to Myshkin, it is not because of his part in the novel but because Ippolit does come close to what he and the others yearn for; viz., a genuine act. This in itself gives him what *Notebooks*' editor Wasiolek calls a "finished character."

Ippolit's suicide does not come off. As it happens with the other characters, the longing to act is frustrated, and he is left with his fever and his loneliness. Yet his attempt is not a "case," since his challenge to the world was a fit response to his hopeless situation and was conceived when he was in full possession of himself. His public declaration, followed by pulling the trigger, would complete his life and define it in its wretched injustice. True, directed against himself, his act would change nothing except the quantity of time allotted him to live, and this emptiness of effect exposes him to the charge of showing off thrown at him by the reluctant witnesses of his performance. But if Ippolit's gesture is not quite an act, it is at least a demonstration, with something in it of finality—in short, as Ippolit himself calls it, a "protest." Even this, however, Dostoyevsky will not grant him; he prefers to drown Ippolit's intensity in a comical accident—his forgetting to insert the firing cap in his revolver—and in the end Ippolit, too, unable to bear the strain of his emotional conflict, falls unconscious and is cheated of his pathos. One might say that Dostoyevsky punishes Ippolit for his self-love in wishing to perform the act that will define him.

It is their awareness of the uncertain ground of their actions that causes the characters of *The Idiot* to hurl themselves toward a decisive event—a marriage, a crime—in the hope that the external situation thus produced will deprive them of choice and impose upon their personalities the unity of fiction. Dostoyevsky introduces reality, with its irresolution, into his novels so that his characters can fight against it. Myshkin, prepared to marry Aglaya or Nastasya, would, once the leap has been taken, be compelled to renounce either love or pity, but his nature is to cling hopelessly to both. To elope with Rogozhin and his gang is for Nastasya a final guarantee of degradation, intended to lead unequivocally to what she calls her "proper place" as a streetwalker. But in Dostoyevsky's universe, any proper place, even at the bottom, is unattainable. Like Ippolit's, Nastasya's final step turns out not to be final; soon she is living with Myshkin in Moscow, and she appears in Pavlovsk among the fast set of the resort as she might have done had she still been Totsky's mistress. To the extent that it was intended to stamp her once and for all, Nastasya's act of self-destruction was not an action at all but a "psychological case," a piece of histrionics, felt yet put on for effect— and she has to perform her decisive act again at her wedding with Myshkin. Action is not accessible to Nastasya; she can do no more than invite Rogozhin's knife. By undermining the deeds of his characters, Dostoyevsky forces us without arguing to assent to Myshkin's belief that "all sinners are sick people."

But though the personae of *The Idiot* are "cases," they are not mad in the ordinary sense—at least, not mad *only* in that sense. Descended from archetypal fictions, their pathology goes deeper than the mere aberrations of individuals. Their maladies are representative; the behavior of a Rogozhin or a Nastasya is an "exaggeration but not by any means a myth." Nastasya is hysterical and self-tormenting, but her dartings to the brink partake of a celebrated style, an aesthetic. Her moods are imposed upon her by the role of the *femme fatale,* the unpredictable lady in black whom men pursue, that she re-creates. Nastasya originated in stories of the innocent virgin fallen under the power of a world-weary sensualist and corrupted by him—a situation psychologically injurious, to be sure, but one glorified also by romantic literature. If Nastasya is mentally ill, it is as a creature of world fiction that she suffers, of poetry, as a universal being remade and recostumed by Russian sensibility. "Whether she was a woman who had read too much poetry, as Radomsky had suggested, or simply mad, as the Prince was convinced," was a matter that could not be settled. But her poetic substance makes her irresistible as one already known and desired before being met, and lifts her madness and that of her lovers into realms of exaltation. Says Totsky, reflectively, as Nastasya departs in Rogozhin's "sledges with bells": "Who would not sometimes be captivated by a woman like that to the point of losing his reason and . . . all the rest?"

The substructure of Dostoyevsky's novels and stories is an extension of the Continental stratum of romantic fiction, with its solitary dreamers, idealistic maidens, self-centered wives, drunken ex-officers, servant girls falsely accused of theft, unexpected legacies. In *The Idiot,* Dostoyevsky develops the insight—already introduced in *Notes from the Underground* and to be harped on later in *The Diary of a Writer*—that this world of introversion and half-serious play acting can no longer sustain great actions, not even the actions of great criminals, but is a breeding ground for hyperdistended egos. The malady of Russia, he finds, lies in the "segregation" of the romantic personality, in the passion of every Russian, the moment he becomes conscious of himself, to possess his own, unique "idea." In opposition to this individualism, imported into nineteenth-century Russia in a decayed condition, *The Idiot* seeks the traces of a new collective substructure of feeling and imagination. Myshkin is the foe of segregation, the apostle of togetherness. During his sojourn in Petersburg and Pavlovsk, people are brought together and confront one another on a deeper plane of understanding, as in the instance of the "astonished footman" to whom Myshkin explains himself upon his initial visit to the Yepanchins, or of Mme Yepanchin lecturing the menacing adolescents seeking justice for Pavlishchev's son. In the Myshkin perspective of social communion, the clairvoyance and uninhibited self-revelation symptomatic of the characters' mental disturbance are transformed into a social promise, as if what is sickness within present human relations will someday be the norm of healthy conduct. You are all "absurd," says Myshkin in a burst of prophetic inspiration before his epileptic collapse, therefore you are "promising material."

Myshkin is, of course, also a lone individual—moreover, one who has come from abroad. "You're overexcited because of your . . . solitary life, perhaps," says the old man at the engagement party, trying to calm him. Myshkin recognizes his isolation but claims, as he is about to be cast down, that he has made a start toward love and happiness. Before the new communion has been achieved, all are sick, including the savior himself. Dostoyevsky can envision no cure for man in his present social condition, only possession by a spirit, or Idea, higher than the forces that now move him—a divine sickness as the alternative to the sickness stemming from the lust for sex or money.

But is there a "high" and a "low" in the domain of the abnormal? Confronted by the question of a hierarchy of metaphysical realms, Dostoyevsky demonstrates the toughness of his realism. For all his will to believe, he refuses to deny nature and take the religious way out. The good and evil effects of extreme experiences cannot always be separated. Meditating on his moments of illumination, Myshkin "often said to himself that all those gleams and flashes of the highest awareness and, hence, also of 'the highest mode of existence,' were nothing but a disease, a departure from the normal condition, and, if so, it was not at all the highest mode of existence but, on the contrary, must be considered to be the lowest." Like Freud and William Blake, Dostoyevsky is prepared to dissolve the distinction between highest and lowest. Myshkin *is* sick, as Rogozhin,

Nastasya, and Ippolit are sick, and all cures are for the future. The measure of their sickness is their "departure from the normal condition"; that is, from the measure of medicine and society. The last word in *The Idiot* is spoken by Mme Yepanchin as she turns from Myshkin, now too far gone to recognize her. "We have had enough of being carried away by our enthusiasms," she asserts, like a Chorus of Sophocles. "It's high time we grew sensible."

Yet, for Dostoyevsky, Myshkin's higher experiences are justified by a value beyond society or its norms, including the norm of health. " 'What if it is a disease?' he [Myshkin] decided at last. 'What does it matter that it is an abnormal tension, if the result, if the moment of sensation, remembered and analyzed in a state of health, turns out to be harmony and beauty brought to their highest point of perfection, and gives a feeling, undivined and undreamt of till then, of completeness, proportion, reconciliation, and an ecstatic and prayerful fusion in the highest synthesis of life?' " In the end, Dostoyevsky's judgment is aesthetic; it is the "Beauty Will Save the World" theme that Aglaya warned Myshkin to avoid at the party. Myshkin's soliloquy on his vision of wholeness is a prose equivalent of Baudelaire's *"ordre et beauté, luxe, calme, et volupté."* The highest attainment of life is not action but a condition of being in which the semi-fictional creatures that govern history give way before a harmony in which time has ceased and in which the instant expands itself indefinitely, as in the inspired state of the artist or in the eternal moment of the victim on the scaffold—that split second in which the epileptic Mohammed had "plenty of time to contemplate all the dwellings of Allah."

6

From Play Acting to Self

"Someone's missing here. It's Sartre." The author of *Being and Nothingness* heard this cry resounding from earth to heaven when as a boy he daydreamed of rescuing maidens in the desert from mustachioed bandits. How he got to be "missing" (and longing, vainly, to be missed) is the subject of *The Words*, Sartre's account of the first ten years of his life. The hero of his history constantly absents himself behind a series of masquerades. In his desert fantasy, young Jean-Paul would "push aside the screen" and bursting into view send heads rolling with his saber. In real life, making himself present was not that easy. It required unceasing struggle with the illusory egos that kept forming themselves in the gaps of his being. This spectral struggle has occupied most of Sartre's life. *The Words* is a negative autobiography, a natural history of the not-selves that crystallized in the time span of the living person and displaced him. No theme, obviously, could be more timely.

Sartre's father died when Jean-Paul was a few months old—the circumstance of having a father unknown to him was responsible, he believes, for the clots of emptiness in his personality. In choosing his son's vocation a father instills in him a sense of purpose. Sartre's father died too soon to be able to give a directing shove to the future of his off-spring. He failed, too, to leave him an inheritance which might have established between them the continuity of things. Thus Sartre's identity was deprived of gravity and left bobbing on the air currents of other people's opinions of him. "A father," he reflects, "would have weighted me with a certain stable obstinacy." As it was, he lived under a constant threat of being blacked out through indifference.

As luck (both good and bad) would have it, he was from his earliest days provided with a dedicated audience. "Rather than the son of a dead man, I was given to understand that I was a child of miracle." Having lost her husband, his youthful mother returned with her infant to the home of her parents. As the pet of Papa Charles Schweitzer, uncle of the celebrated Albert, Sartre grew up in an environment of middle-class refinement and conceit. The little outsider quickly learns how to win applause by palming himself off as a cultural asset. Having no incentive to do, he performs. His mother, once more fallen under the parental system, is like an older sister, who coddles him and coaches his performance as the star of the family. His grandfather dotes on him and eagerly connives in deceptions calculated to prove him the ancestor of a prodigy ("what he worshipped in me was his generosity"). Sartre's childish utterances are read as oracles; he elicits wonder through deliberate fabrications of nonsense. The little hipster aims to please and finds "nothing more amusing than to play at being good." At four he is an accomplished comedian who "never cries and hardly laughs." Later, having taught himself to read, he delights himself in solitude with juvenile thriller magazines, while he continues to draw gasps in the drawing room for his pretended devotion to the classics. This double life is summed up in *The Words* with the force of a proposition of Descartes: "I led two lives, both of them untrue."

Short, growing up unhandsome, Sartre found in language the chief materials for his impostures and his self-substitutions. Through words, "the little faker" put himself in the spotlight that gilded his "uncalled-for" life. In words, too, he discovered a universe that matched his own immateriality, which he could enjoy at will and even control. The encyclopedia surrounded him with plants, butterflies and heroes—actual creatures would remain crude approximations of those first met on the page. Without friends or antagonists, the phrase-made darling gesticulated in a setting of labels. *The Words* does not hesitate to confess that the wish "to live in the ether among simulacra of Things" influenced Sartre's later political conceptions.

In the fantasy world of reading, Sartre encountered the semi-fabulous personage, the Great Writer, whose image was to rule his life. To the child, an author and his books were one: Corneille had a leather back; this gave him the added merit of substantiality. Becoming a writer himself was with Sartre a new, powerful means of showing off for his claque—"above all, I wrote because I was Charles Schweitzer's grandson." Yet putting words on paper and assuming the poses of an author (in secret, as well as for the visitors whom his mother brought tiptoeing in to watch him at his desk) carried him into a realm different from mere reading. Writing was an activity able to hold its shape in the material world; thus it began to give shape to an "I" that existed apart from the responses of its public. Instead of losing himself as formerly in his pulp-fiction imaginings, Sartre found he could project his desires into heroes from whom he kept himself apart. Splitting off characters from himself implied a unique remainder that was he. At the same time he discovered that he had the power to make things happen to his creations for which he might have to hold himself responsible. " 'Daisy ran her hand over her eyes,' " he had written. " 'She had become blind.' That easy to be wicked! I sat there stunned." Through fiction he was learning to question his motives and his morals.

In the activity of writing there became manifest the glimmering of a self. Sartre's torment, however, was that he not only wrote but assumed the role of writer. Literary eminence had been predicted for him by the family and its friends and he accommodatingly cast himself for the part. The classic author-to-be stood as a changeless eidolon against the developing personality of the boy of ten. One whose future has been foreseen lives only to fill in the details (Sartre fails to note the analogy between obeying the preconceived plot of his life and obeying the Marxist-Leninist plot of history). Long before he could execute a work, Sartre suffered to the full the anxiety of the artist to make every moment of his existence a contribution to the ultimate catalogue of his creations. He lived in order to provide material for his future biographer. Sartre's prose rises to almost biblical excoriation as he recites how the literary "mandate" that was lodged in him voided his daily life of the savor of immediacy. "My future eternity became my concrete future: it made every instant trivial, it was at the core of the deepest attention, it was an even deeper state of abstraction, it was the emptiness of all plenitude, the light unreality of reality; it killed from a distance the taste of a caramel in my mouth, the sorrows and pleasures in my heart." Railroaded toward his goal, already fully achieved in the groundplan of his sensibility, Sartre was too well armored against novelty; nothing that befell his person could alter the enactment of the script that had been written for him. "Chance events did not exist: I was involved only with their providential counterfeits." His life had been formulated in advance of being lived and real happenings had to be excluded from it. In sum, Sartre was living in a myth, like Oedipus or like the proletariat in the scheme of Marx's philosophy of history.

By gliding in among the immortals of literature, the sly, unneeded good boy had contrived to satisfy a wish to die ("the true meaning of all my gestures") without giving offense to his adoring family. The impulse that changed Ionesco's protagonist into a rhinoceros transformed Sartre into a statue. In both, metamorphosis was a well-behaved means of taking leave of life. The image of the studious kid posed in the marble ranks of Sophocles, Ovid, Racine, Hugo, Jean-Paul Sartre, "one of whom was still alive," is authentically Chaplinesque. Indeed, the picture presented in *The Words* of death-dealing family life is not unlike that in *Monsieur Verdoux,* whose hero, also thoroughly domesticated, simply carried marriage to its logical conclusion before it could breed would-be suicides. Apparently inspired by truths attainable only with a dagger, Sartre's writing has never before been so witty. "My father's insolent disease had displeased the Schweitzers; it looked too much like a repudiation. My mother was deemed guilty of not having foreseen or forestalled it. She had thoughtlessly taken a husband who had not worn well." "Those proud, modest bourgeois were of the opinion that beauty was beyond their means or beneath their station; it was all right for a marquise or a whore."

Yet *The Words* is a settling of accounts not with others but with himself and with the complicated game of absconding which his childhood forced him to invent as a defense against despair, and which he went on playing until almost yesterday. That this act of self-recognition takes the form of comedy (one is also reminded by *The Words* of Sascha Guitry's *Story of a Cheat*) represents a remarkable leap in Sartre's imagination over his earlier fiction.

It is plain to Sartre that his urge toward salvation was essentially religious. His decision to become a writer belonged to an experience of secular conversion ("I thought I was devoting myself to literature, whereas I was actually taking Holy Orders") that put his family at a distance, lifted him into an order above time, and imposed upon him a ready-made self that he could live up to only through repeated acts of creation and self-cancellation. This substitute religion with its content of glory and death became for Sartre the final antagonist. In his writing he was once again doomed to be "missing" unless he could resist the bait of immortality that drove him to write (committed to this point of view, how could he fail to reject the Nobel Prize?). Worse still, the missing Sartre made Sartre a perpetual trickster. As a secretly elected immortal he could realize his mission by writing eloquently about the impossibility of realizing missions. It is against such devitalizing ambiguities of the chosen that *The Words* is directed. Its aim is not to reconstitute the past (the usual one of autobiography) but to dissolve those residues of transcendence which have nailed the author to the wall.

Sartre goes to the extreme in repudiating traits of his character which might have derived from his ghostly privilege of genius. "Fake to the marrow of my bones and hoodwinked, I joyfully wrote about our unhappy state." To be hoodwinked (*"mystifié"*) would seem to absolve one to some degree from being fake. But if Sartre is now exaggerating his past deceptions, it is because he has in *The Words* embarked on a new mission: to root out any ruse by which he might be engaged in saving himself. He wishes to be vulnerable to the diurnal, to be "a traveler without a ticket." From a devotee of God under intellectually respectable disguises, he has become a mystic of the living instant, of the new, "ushered in this very hour but . . . never instituted: tomorrow everything goes by the board."

This conversion to "atheism" was also a purging of class, since, in Sartre's judgment, his rushing forward into the empty outline of his eternal renown was an expression of the middle-class ideals of abstract progress and success. Writing *The Words* brought this surge to a halt and changed him into himself. It was an incantation pronounced against the spell in which the Sleeping (Non-) Beauty had been held for half a century. Its negative movement carried out an act of self-liberation and self-discovery. Sartre's childhood had determined him to be a writer, and it was now too late for silence. But one can work in words without taking on the comedy of the literary man, his costume, his conceits, his superiority, his silly hopes of rising above mortality through his creations. An air of Ecclesiastes settles over the final pages of *The Words*. "For the last ten years or so I've been a man who's been waking up, cured of a long, bitter-sweet madness, and who can't get over the fact, a man who can't think of his old ways without laughing and who doesn't know what to do with himself." Salvation? It is enough to break through to living—no longer to be someone who's missing.

Sartre's conclusion that his abstract role playing was in reality a barrier against death is identical with the conception of Tolstoy in *The Death of Ivan Ilych*. Sartre, however, is more modest philosophically than Tolstoy and more appealing—he takes the burden of self-falsification upon himself in the particular conditions of his upbringing instead of projecting it, as Tolstoy did, as a criticism of civilized man. If Ilych is an actor, Sartre is an actor conscious that he is acting. Sartre is also of the mid-twentieth century in that he sees the issue of his new-found trust in sheer living to be one not of belief but of experience and behavior—while with Tolstoy resignation to death became an ideological tool, designed to win converts to his version of Christianity. Sartre refuses to make intellectual use of his death-accepting self but demands of it nothing less than that it supply him with continual surprises.

On the other hand, Sartre is more nostalgic than Tolstoy, more a man of the book, and he feels himself deprived as he imagines that others—for example, the boys at the lycée with whom he ran yelling around the Place du Panthéon—touched textures of reality that eluded him. That is why Sartre's tone is sad, despite his new-found exhilaration at being released from hope. If Tolstoy's life before his "awakening" was a fictional construct, it was one in the full Byzantine color of action and poetry. Sartre's life, like his literary style, is marked by the even grayness of prose. In confessing how he hid himself under masks, *The Words* says nothing of his ever having been carried beyond himself by an adventure, an idea, a masterpiece. Sartre is a singular product of a crossing of academic and popular culture. The typical flaws in his writing are overabstraction and melodrama. "I plunged into pride and sadism, in other words, into generosity, which, like avarice or race prejudice, is only a secret balm for healing our inner wounds and which ends by poisoning us."

Proust threw himself back into a past that was waiting for him. For Sartre only the future waited, and his task was to derange it so he could avoid keeping the appointment. Given this attitude toward time, how could he compose an autobiography, which is a looking back? While in substance *The Words* starts conventionally with the birth of the author, in form it is oddly circular. The boy was what he was because he was imagining himself to be Sartre, or someone like him. And Sartre is what he is because the boy brought him to life in his imagination, though at fifty-nine he has managed to make himself different from the adult that inhabited the boy. But the boy and the man lack continuity and cannot come into contact. "Above all, no promiscuity: I keep my past at a respectful distance." There are two circles—the boy completing himself in the adult stranger and the man in the rejected boy—and the circles are concentric. Sartre had to break into his past like (if one may be forgiven the pun) a second-story man.

The Words revolutionizes the form of autobiography by destroying the notion of a one-way progression from earlier to later phenomena. One might, adapting Freud, call it a case study in The Dramapathology of Everyday Life. In it the formation of human personality begins with the individual finding himself on a stage and forced to conceive a part in an unknown plot. The dynamics of development consists in working through fiction into reality, from play acting to the self. "The playing at culture," writes Sartre, "cultivated me in the long run." Very likely, this differentiation between the actor self and the natural self is too schematic, too theatrical. Every action contains an element of imitation, that is, of fiction; to escape being an "actor" one would have to be utterly passive. Sartre, in sum, is still starting with words rather than with realities. Having executed his fearless striptease, he imagines that he has quit the theater of the self forever. The chances are much greater that he is between the acts. Since he is one of the most original performers of the century, the impossibility of his leaving the stage is not to be deeply regretted.

7

Criticism-Action

We have to go back to the
witch doctors or to the Shakespeare of *Hamlet* or *Macbeth*
to reach a world in which spectres, abstract beings, names
come to life, "objective powers" play so large a part as they
do in that of Marx—from that "mysterious thing," the
commodity, which floats in the shadow of the physical
products of modern industry, to those "personifications of
economic relations," the social classes, which, according to
Capital, are the protagonists of the political economic
drama. Each of these entities, in one of Marx's most characteristic phrases, "takes on an independent existence over
against the individuals" and dominates human behavior.
It is they who supply both the actors and the props for the
stage of history; living men and women, magically bound
to their service as Caliban by the wand of Prospero, act but
to effect *their* ends. Even the hero, Marx takes pains to
demonstrate, while imagining that he follows his own will,
actually sustains in his thought and feeling the mode of
life, the limits and half-conscious purposes of a collective
person, the class which has chosen him, and he is lifted up

or cast down according to its condition and stage of development.

With Marx, of course, these incorporeal figures and powers have not migrated into the human sphere from nature or the supernatural; they are offsprings of men's own activities, and precisely of the most practical. They are concretions of behavior as it has been given its shape within the social whole; phantom as they are, they are inseparable from human reality. For instance, a social class for Marx is an "illusory community," but it arises from and embodies the most basic relations, the "materialist connection of men with one another." A class is composed entirely of alter egos, since individuals "belong to it only as average individuals" and not as unique persons; yet this community of doubles is the individual's exclusive ground of self-realization. For Marx the ruling principle of civilized life is metamorphosis, in which nothing is real except in its transfictional state.

We hesitate to call "myth" this system of constructs which are not merely mental but the specific forms of the human world. "The difference," says Marx, "between the individual as person and what is accidental to him is not a conceptual difference but an historical fact. This distinction has a different significance at different times." Nevertheless, we cannot avoid speaking of these changing creations in metaphors of the imaginary. In history, as in the dream, past actions come to life again in current happenings, and these residues keep the living present at a distance. This deprivation of an immediate, waking contact with things and events, this lack of the direct savor of life, is the common impoverishment. Our acts as clerks, mechanics, professors or radical critics encase us as if they had molded themselves in clay or metal upon our bodies. The tyranny of the done causes our very skills to frustrate our purposes, like that knife thrower of De Maupassant who had become so expert he could not miss his target even when his life depended on it. Man makes himself against himself. *"Le mort saisit le vif,"* Marx recites in the Preface to *Capital*.

But it is not only the survival of anachronisms that Marx wishes to combat. Capitalism, he believes, is attending to this task. Marx is not slow to celebrate the tremendous physical onslaught of capitalism against all traditional forms and institutions, as well as the scientific criticism it has applied to ancient superstitions. "Constant revolutionizing of production, uninterrupted disturbance of all social conditions, everlasting uncertainty and agitation, distinguish the bourgeois epoch from all earlier ones. All fixed, fast-frozen relations, with their train of ancient and venerable prejudices and opinions, are swept away, all new-formed ones become antiquated before they can ossify." The single individual has emerged and has declared his independence, claiming his association with others to be the result of a free contract.

Capitalism, however, has not broken the siege of the past upon the present. It has banished religious fetishes only to succumb to *a process of fetish-making* of its own. Bourgeois society was itself born out of myth, explains *The Eighteenth Brumaire;* the revolutions that brought it into being summoned up personages, costumes and rhetoric out of long-vanished states. Most important, it has established as its essential activity the conversion of living human energy into spectral force—for to Marx that is just what *capital* is, a quasi-*thing* that incorporates the past actions of men and women and is thus able to control what they do now. "In bourgeois society, living labor is but a means to increase accumulated labor . . . in bourgeois society therefore the past dominates the present." Folded in the center of capitalist dynamics Marx detected a stasis in which completed being embodied itself continually.

It is toward this motionless center, from which emanate like steam from a crack the Delphic wraiths of capitalism, that *Capital* directs its tremendously detailed, systematic analysis. Assuming in the form of capital a fierce mechanical vitality, the dead labor of men extends in every direction a web of abstract entities that control the world as if in obedience to a will of their own. Marx's major work sets itself the task to translate these magical excrescences back into their human matter. Behind the system of "independent existents"—the commodity, money, the market—*Capital* exposes the processes by which expended labor is converted into the economic plasm which is the source of capitalist vigor; and it outlines the drama of class coercion, spiritual poverty and revolt that accompanies that conversion. The bias for this exposure is Marx's unlimited hostility to mystification and his stubborn belief in the immediate possibility of a society in which, as in the communism described in *The German Ideology,* it will be "impossible that anything shall exist independently of individuals, insofar as things are only a product of the preceding intercourse of the individuals themselves."

The effigies of the unalive (money, etc.) rule both inside the mind and in the physical organization of society—to expel them and attain to individual life their independent existence, and with it their superhuman power, must be destroyed in both. All criticism, Marx had written early, is criticism of religion, and criticism and revolution complement each other. By demonstrating how capital, the commodity, property, are actually frozen human acts and relations, criticism dissolves these deities in the consciousness and makes the description of them contingent on the history of classes. In turn, by demonstrating how social classes are actually compounded out of changing modes of producing subsistence, criticism destroys the illusion of the independence of these collective egos and makes them contingent on economic behavior and the material world. The evolution of class struggles, Marx wrote to Wedemeyer in 1852, had been described by others before him, as had, too, the economic physiology of classes: his own contribution, he said, rested on three propositions, the first of which was: "that the existence of classes was tied up with certain phases of material production." If inside the economic system operated the human drama of class compulsion and resistance, inside the bodies of the classes circulated the routines by which real men kept themselves alive. To carry out a double unmasking, peeling economic abstraction from human abstraction in order to reach the facts from which all social abstractions have grown, is the innovation of materialist criticism. In everything "the root is man."

In Marx's dialectics, events themselves are an unmasking; the uncovering of reality takes place not in the mind alone but through an actual corporeal stripping off of the social and historical "integument"—another characteristic expression—which makes the human fact what it is. History is like the tragedy of the Greeks: behind the present fact on the stage there exists the hidden fact, which is coming out and will be recognized through its inevitable enactment. Without the tragic enactment, criticism is only an opinion. By itself, in the absence of a change in the situation, it can never win lasting conviction, for the "unreal" fact stands forth to contradict it. Evidences of the evils of capitalism are answered by evidences of the great benefits it has brought to mankind. Since the source of social myth is the real relations of society, the mere critic of existing forms is doomed to be the hero of a fable of frustration. Every false image the exasperated modern Tiresias laboriously scrapes from the brain of his auditors is restored without delay by data generated in the factories and streets. If criticism is not to be an end in itself, it must be a means to put an end to those material conditions from which mirage is bred—"those conditions whose life-principle has already been refuted" but which survive nevertheless as a fetter upon life. "In themselves," Marx complains with a note of the boredom of the philosopher with the lag of existence, "they are not sufficiently worthy of attention but are a state of fact both despicable and despised." The aim of materialist analysis is not to carry on an endless unveiling of particular examples of animated death but to help eliminate all of them by laying bare their common social cause to a stroke of force.

Criticism, then, for Marx is an action. More exactly, it is the beginning of an action; one that demands completion by social transformation. It is in regard to the latter phase of attack upon the myth content of modern civilization, that part of the action-criticism that has to be carried out by others than the critic, that the great practical problems of Marx's thought arise, including those of its political strategy and its ethics—and with these the related questions of the revolutionary roles of the individual, the political party and the social class.

For Marx, the assault of criticism upon the "objective powers" is to be made effective by the revolution of a class, the proletariat. If, as has been maintained, Christian philosophy differs from the pagan in that it centers upon a unique event of the past, the Crucifixion, Marx's historical materialism distinguishes itself equally from all other philosophies in centering on the future victory of the working class. In his letter to Wedemeyer cited above, Marx enumerates two further innovations of his thought, in addition to his explanation of classes: the idea of the *necessary* conquest of power by the proletariat, and that of the function of that power in ending the class struggle by bringing to life a society of free individuals. At the heart of Marxism is its contention that its criticism and the revolutionary action of the working class have the identical objective, that revolution by the second is the material equivalent of the first and supplies its positive social content. This daring concept, whatever be its scientific validity, is a precondition for thinking as a Marxist.

Was the correspondence between materialist criticism and working-class striving for power to be the result of the adoption by a decisive quantity of individual workingmen of Marx's theories? The answer is, definitely, No. Apart from his contempt for ideologists and Utopians, including "Marxists," who see in ideas the cause of historical happenings, Marx's entire perspective excludes the notion that an historical effect can originate with an individual or an association of individuals. The conqueror of classes and of class struggle must itself be one of history's collective pseudo-organisms, a class. The action of the proletariat paralleling materialist criticism was to be self-motivated as a necessary result both of the nature of the proletariat and of the objective conditions stimulating it to revolt.

To qualify the working class for its meta-critical role, Marx evoked the negative processes of capitalism which, in denuding the proletariat of illusory being, must cause their revolutionary action to come forth as an accurate expression of their situation and to guide them with ever-deepening clarity. Primarily, the unique competence of this class to attain to the real arises from the utter futility of the daily acts of the factory laborers in conferring individuality upon themselves. They exist as an incorporation of generality. If all men belong to their respective classes only as "average individuals," with the proletarian, "average" is the whole of what he is. His time is a wage rate, his psychic product not a self but an interchangeable commodity.

Thus in the modern worker, Marx contends, the difference between the individual person and his class has been suppressed, and with it the illusory nature of both. Members of all other historical classes, split by the division of labor, have achieved their existence in the masquerade of types compounded by society out of their traditional activities—aristocrat, court jester, peasant. In the proletariat capitalism has created the very personification of self-emptying through social behavior, those "newfangled men," as Marx called them, who, like the machine, are "an invention of modern times" and are multiplied automatically with the accumulation of capital. With the worker the social process of appropriating the individual's past and using it to dominate his present has been carried to its extreme. Since his work assumes the form of capital which is taken away from him, he is constantly drained of his "life content"; his acts produce no accretion of individuality, not even an illusory one. On the contrary, the products which are the substance of his being are in their transmuted form applied only to extract more labor from him.* Wrung dry on this wheel of both his past time and his living time, of both memory and imagination, the worker exists as an "abstract individual."

But by the very fact that the workingmen are through their productive activity constantly rendered into human nothings, Marx sees them as "put into a position to enter into relations with one another as *individuals*" (his emphasis) and to act together in the daylight of genuine self-

---

* *Capital* in describing this process resorts to melodramatic language: "Capital is dead labor, that vampire-like only lives by sucking living labor, and lives the more the more labor it sucks."

interest. No past, personal or class, no socially constructed self, complete with costume, rhetoric and beliefs, stands between the factory worker and his fellows, nor between his sense of community and the reality on which it is based. If he begins to act for himself, his act will be a genuine self-expression, at the same time that it will be an act for all. "Only the proletariat of the present day, who are completely shut off from all self-activity, are in a position to achieve a complete and no longer restricted self-activity."

But the workers cannot act for themselves without breaking the social mechanism which transforms their acts into commodities and siphons them off as capital, that is, without a revolution against the living source of modern hallucination, capitalism. Hence the choice stated by Marx—"The working class is either revolutionary or it is nothing"—is the formula both for his own critique of capitalism as a specific epoch in the history of human alienation, and for the impulse of the workers to revolution as a revulsion against the void within them. Whenever a crisis of capitalism reproduces the vacuity of the proletariat as physical hunger and the direct threat of death, the *final* revolution is on the order of the day.

By his revolutionary action the worker starts a psychic increment that makes him an individual; he arrives, as Rosa Luxemburg emphasized, at ethical existence. The appearance of this class upon the stage of history brings new persons into the world (not molecules of a mass), whose characters are derived from the single social activity that cannot harden into a thing, from revolution. The restoration of alienated labor would destroy these persons, in destroying their freedom; hence the condition of their survival is the "revolution in permanence." The new existence itself of the workingmen depends on their day-by-day triumph over surplus value as a social force against each;

and this victorious existence, constantly augmenting individuality, is itself socialism and the "transition to the abolition of all classes."

For Marx, therefore, the socialist revolution is immanent in the nature of the proletarian class and the need of its human components to achieve individuality. On the other hand, *apart from their intellectual struggle against mystification,* individuals as such have no deciding role in the historical drama; their free action can begin only *at the end of history* and with the vanishing of classes.

Materialist criticism is the revolutionary action of the individual; revolutionary activity is materialist criticism by the working class. Marx's conviction of the interrelation and the inevitable synchronization of these two processes constitutes the key to his politics and assigns to individuals and the class their different roles in it. The Communists, whether they consisted exclusively of Marx and Engels or of an association that multiplied the Marxian voice, were not, according to *The Communist Manifesto,* to form a separate group competing with other working-class parties for control of proletarian action. Their revolutionary function was to carry on the double unmasking of materialist criticism: "in all political movements they bring to the front as the leading question in each the property question, no matter what its degree of development at the time," showing changes in the relations of production to be at once the means and the end of the transformation of society. Conversely, in all social and economic questions, they expose the content of class coercion and struggle. Taking for granted the growing organization, cohesion and will to combat of the proletariat, spontaneously brought about by the processes of capitalist production, Marxian criticism would act upon the proletarian revolution in two ways: (1) As the "head of passion" it would help change instinctive action into conscious action by bringing before the workingmen the formulation of their position and of their experience as a class; (2) as the irreconcilable challenge of the mind to mystification, it would provide a model of suspicion and hostility toward bourgeois society, a sentry for the class of workingmen against delusions through which they might be made a tool to defeat their own interests.

So long as it assumes that it is operating in the presence of rising proletarian revolt, Marxian criticism is an action that remains criticism. Where, however, its intellectual attack against existing society no longer takes for granted the parallel movement of the victim class, a terrifying confusion besets Marxism, particularly with regard to the historical roles of individuals and classes. Its political concepts and social values become ambiguous, or even appear in reverse. Personalities, parties, ideas become all at once prodigies of history-making and responsible day by day for the destiny of man.

In theory unwavering as to the revolutionary capacity of the proletariat, Marx was not tempted to put criticism into a position inferior to action. For him the plot of history was given, including its dénouement. The process by which labor is converted into capital also holds the secret of capitalism's future wreck: using its transportable energy, capital, it continually augments both the class of wage workers and the productive power of labor by creating a constantly widening interplay of men and tools, at the same time that, through the accumulation and centralization of wealth, it narrows the slit through which this growing force must pass in order to be changed into capital. An ever-mounting pressure, ever more closely confined—and which is reflected in the tensions of the classes, their preparations, their strategies. In the explosion which is inevitable, unless alert popular forces create the means for bringing about socialization by stages, the cave of illusions vanishes and labor is left in the open air of the free cooperation of individuals.

This prediction, that capitalism must automatically develop the elements of the society that will supersede it, presents, of course, the famous "contradiction" in Marx between the inevitability of socialism and the call to revolution. It is pragmatism, however, not Marx that sees the historical protagonists as free individuals needing the stimulation of an undetermined end in order to strive for a social form which they have chosen. In Marx's own terms, which allow for no interval of individual contemplation and decision outside the drama of history, the so-called contradiction is meaningless. If the "higher powers" that combat each other existed entirely separate from us, we could passively await their self-destruction. If, on the other hand, they were mere images, analysis could dissolve them like the superstitions left over from dead societies. Since, however, classes and their phantom by-products both control our behavior as external powers and live in us as ourselves, our lives *are* the actions we take with regard to them. We need no desired outcome to induce us to fight the class struggle—the struggle fights us. And if the Marxist critic wills the victory of the proletariat, it is not for the sake of the future of others but from the necessity of his own present thought. His intellectual effort is a resistance to the shapes of nightmare, a resistance which the conviction that waking is near does not weaken. History is the action of mass "I's," and since the command to act is always present, the action of individuals is a species of passivity to the same degree as is their abstention from action. Even hesitation is an action, as in *Hamlet;* for Marx, hesitation and vacillation are the typical actions of the lower bourgeoisie as the class pressed between classes. In a profound sense, Marx's view dissolves the aura of grandeur and irrationality of the historical activist and his tendency to revolutionary conceit.

Concentrating on the mass actors of the historical drama, Marx was not interested in the political choices of individuals but only in the accuracy with which their views and their acts mirrored the hidden movements of the social process—an instance is his well-known admiration of the royalist Balzac in contrast to his scorn for socialist litterateurs. The moral issue of individual adherence (and betrayal), which has taken on so much importance in the parliamentary and conspiratorial Marxism of this century, is irrelevant to Marx's conception of historical change; one looks in vain in his writings for reflections on the psychology or ethics of individual identification with party or class. When he himself takes part in organizational activities, it is exclusively as the promoter of his own ideas. Nor does the absence of a political agency in which to work cause his efforts to lapse; the proletarian mass hero must wait for favorable conditions, including his own inner development. The critic need not wait; his exposures constitute an intellectual equivalent of the situation and by that very fact are a force for changing it. Nowhere is there a hint in Marx of a wish to change himself or to add ethical density to his existence through revolutionary commitment. Since a man's intellectual products, like those of his manual skills, stand against him as an alien force, Marx does not expect his ideas to result in a clarification of his own personality, and, as noted, "Marxist" is to him a derogatory term. Communism could not be for him either a discipline of self-effacement or a means of self-definition, as it has been for such activists as Malraux and Brecht, and the question of to be or not to be a Communist is never addressed by him either to himself or to others.

With the loss of its metaphysical assurance and with its admission of doubt regarding the political capacity of the proletariat and its destiny—a doubt upon which were founded both the absent-minded revisionist socialism of Bernstein and elite activism of Lenin—Marxism has seen its synthesis of criticism and action split into separate parts that enter into conflict with each other. For Marx, as we have seen, the intellectual exposure of the material realities that are cloaked in political concepts, mass beliefs, etc., is inevitably accompanied by a social force that is preparing to change them. But no sooner does Marxism itself turn into an ideology designed to unite the actions of individuals than it abandons its critical position and with it its dialectical relation to social transformation. The Party as the association of Marxian professionals stands as an independent power against both the class of laborers and the individuals that belong to the Party. The discontinuity of the mass "I" of the proletariat, its rise from and relapse into nothingness, which is the pathetic basis of its experience of itself, as well as the impetus of its future freedom, is eliminated through the displacement of the class by the Party leaders, for whom revolutionary politics exists as a profession. In place of resistance to deprivation that converts itself into political action, acceptance of the Party program by individual workers becomes the form of working-class unity. With the lifeless discipline of the machine and the appropriation of his productive energies extended into the political realm, the worker remains set fast in his abstractness, a personification of nullity decked out with Marxist slogans.

At the same time, working-class revolt, since it is no

longer a reflex of the workers' situation, ceases to serve as a revelation of the internal stresses of society, so that revolutionary criticism is deprived of the data by which to correct itself. The Party as idea and as collective force becomes fixed in the mind of the revolutionist as his illusory character. From being an effort to repulse the unreal, revolution becomes a surrender to a fetishism of the historical act—once again a product of the human brain, this time History appears as endowed with its own life and capable of entering into transactions with human beings. The Party (and its foes) take on the appearance of being infinitely active, while the working class and the individual Communist repeatedly collapse into apathy and are blamed for the Party's failures. Needless to add, the critical activities of individuals, the only historical initiative available to them as such, are systematically extinguished. For all their pretense of "activating" the masses, modern revolutionary parties promote an enormous passivity.

Marxism as a system is unthinkable apart from its promise of proletarian victory and its all-liberating effects. It is a philosophy suspended upon an event, a monologue in the drama of history which can be saved from being a soliloquy only by the action of its mass hero. The human content of Marxism, the future toward which it aspires, is to be found not in its own formulas but in the creative innovations to be undertaken by the huge shadow at its side: "The great social measure of the Commune," said Marx in *The Civil War in France,* "was its own working existence."

No one is a Marxist who does not anticipate the proletarian transformation of society and strive to bring it about as the means for putting the demons to flight. Contrariwise, no one is a Marxist who, in the presumed interest of working-class liberation, consents to serve the powers of the new other world created by Marxist totalitarianism. If Marx's proletarian solution to human alienation proves to be a mirage, if the promise in his thought of a leap into a clarified consciousness must be canceled, Marxism is dead, however many clues may still be found in the Marxian tradition for building novel strategies of power upon apathetic masses.

But with or without Marxism, what remains valid in Marx's thinking is the model it provides of persistent social unmasking—precisely the function of which hallucinatory communism deprives it. Nor has Marx's criticism of capitalist society as centering upon the human void of wage labor and commodity production (though from the point of view of Marx this criticism cannot surmount the impotence of mere criticism) lost its pertinence, so long as the processes that produce a proletariat continue to operate. Marx's criticism may even be indispensable for grasping the situation presented by proletarian *non-action*.

For Marx, the consequence of the failure of the proletariat to act in the face of the advancing collectivization of production could be nothing else than "barbarism," the proliferation of a modern Darkest Africa of unreal beings, sacred abstractions, secular cults, illusory communities. Will anyone deny that bad dreams and farces have become typical of public life, to say nothing of private? Is it necessary to demonstrate that these phenomena have to do with the processes of depersonalization and passivity through one's vocation which Marx described as "proletarianization"? With the expanding social organization of production, with private accumulation growing increasingly rare, with the deepening dependence and inner isolation of individuals, the psychic condition of the nineteenth-century factory worker has, despite the proportionate decline in the quantity of such workers, become more and more the rule in twentieth-century society. Abstract man multiplies; a progressive flattening of personality takes place, irrespective of salary categories, standards of living, bureaucratic rank. Demoralized by their strangeness to themselves and by their lack of control over their relations with others, members of every class surrender themselves to artificially constructed mass egos that promise to restore their links with the past and the future. Instead of the self-creating revolt of nothings at the base of society, history appears to hold out a horror Utopia of universal de-individualization headed by leaders who *are* their masks. Within this half-formed world of real spectres, Marx's criticism of modern industrial society as centered on the proletarian void offers at least a conceptual foothold. The weapon of criticism is undoubtedly inadequate. Who on that account would choose to surrender it?

8

Actor in History

In a famous argument with Trotsky in 1931, André Malraux maintained that his novel *The Conquerors,* which dealt with events of the Chinese Revolution, was "first of all a presentation of the human condition." By this he meant that he had dramatized the political struggle in the Far East as a version of the age-old struggle of human beings against hunger and physical mistreatment. Malraux's revolutionary heroes knew that the primal misery was not going to be resolved through their deeds; they fought not for an idea or a cause but in order to join in the combat of Man the oppressed; they died not for any concrete objective but in reaction against the universal pain and humiliation. This pathos of Malraux's heroes was shared by the cowards and brutes; they, too, were reacting against insult and injury, as exemplified by the torturer König in *Man's Fate,* who became what he was through being beaten half dead by the Reds. That Malraux's characters fought on while convinced of their ultimate defeat gave their actions the dimensions of tragedy.

The perspective of the human condition, Malraux felt,

exposed the limitations of other strategies for coping with the political problems of our time. "A Marxist act," Malraux advised Trotsky, "is only possible as a function of class consciousness"—and class consciousness only comes into being in people who have lived under particular conditions of production and education. Hong, the revolutionist in *The Conquerors,* was not a Marxist, Malraux said; he was a man who had emerged "from misery" (not, Malraux might have added, from *Das Kapital*): "he does not care a fig for the future of the proletariat. The proletariat interests him only in its heroism. . . . His aim is ethical, not political, and it is hopeless." Hong's heritage of misery and his ethical will, Malraux thought, gave him a deeper understanding of the twentieth century than that of any Party member and perhaps of Trotsky too.

That Malraux should speak of a "Marxist act" is interesting. For a Marxist, of course, all acts are "Marxist"—Bonaparte's as well as Lenin's—in that they are factors in history as interpreted by Marxist theory. Malraux, however, conceives ideas not as modes of understanding but as attitudes leading to particular styles of behavior. The substance of an idea is not its truth but the act which is its "function." This rule applies to Malraux's own conception of the human condition: it is not a mere statement for philosophical contemplation. It is a "position," a dramatic stance. It introduces into the contemporary political and intellectual scene a new persona, the representative of man's eternal lot. The hopeless hero of history competes dramatically not only with the "Marxist actor" (identified by Malraux with the agents of the Comintern whom he first met in the Orient in the twenties) but also with the agents of international capital, the Falangist, the Liberal, the Anarchist.

In Malraux's novels, as in his writings on art, the personification of man's ineluctable defeat holds the center of the stage, setting the tone for a variety of lost types who gesticulate in an atmosphere of glamorous resignation. And by the side of his hero, Malraux himself, in the guise of a man enacting Man, has played his part in the major situations of the past forty years.

Thus while Malraux is both an artist and a theoretician, he is above all a protagonist. He speaks as a character seeking to give his own stamp to the historical drama in which all who live in this epoch have taken part. He has striven to bring his art and his thought into play with actual events. His ideas have been both instigators of real actions and their verbal accompaniment.

Since Malraux's writings are part of his total performance, they ought to be interpreted in the light of it. Words like "Man," "Action," "Solidarity," "History" take their meanings from the use to which he has put them within the framework of contemporary conflicts. What is "Fate" to one who has found necessity embodied in the Communist Party—and who has obeyed that necessity while declaiming that communism would not lead to the salvation of man? A question of this kind cannot be answered by general discourses on the destiny of man. To discuss Malraux's theories and fiction apart from what their author has been doing, including the doing of his words, is like discussing a character in a play by analyzing his dialogue without paying attention to his part in the plot. Perhaps a special kind of historic-dramatic criticism is needed to deal with a writer who has intended not only to capture our attention as an artist but to change our lives as a political force. In forming an opinion of his creations, the critic would have to bring into focus his own convictions concerning the happenings and issues which he shared with the author as his contemporary.

Typical Malraux criticism, however, at least that available in the United States, treats Malraux as a philosopher and poet of human destiny, whose part in the history of the drama of our time is no more relevant in evaluating his work than might be the fact that an author had been employed in a bank. "Malraux is interested in art but he is also interested in man," wrote Maurice Blanchot. This statement, with its stress on aesthetics and philosophy, is quoted as the first sentence of *Malraux*, an anthology of essays edited by Professor R. W. B. Lewis, and its note of timeless universality is maintained throughout the entire collection. Except for Trotsky's criticism of *The Conquerors*, referred to at the beginning of this essay, and Edmund Wilson's brief notice in the early thirties misconstruing *Man's Fate* as indicating Malraux's development toward Marxism, the critics in *Malraux* address themselves to the lofty plane of the human condition not only, as Malraux proposed, "first of all," but exclusively and to the end. In his Introduction, Professor Lewis deplores the failure of some writers to comprehend Malraux's passionate hostility to limitations. The first selection in his book, by Professor W. M. Frohock, declares that "*Man's Fate* is not just a novel about an insurrection"; its secondary characters, "as well as the protagonist, mirror the universal fate of man." Frohock had noted elsewhere that *Man's Hope*, however, may have been meant as propaganda in behalf of the Loyalist cause in the Spanish Civil War. For this he is roundly rebuked in the contribution of Professor Joseph Frank. "Nothing could be further from the truth," asserts the latter; "the whole purpose of *Man's Hope* is to portray the tragic dialectic between means and ends inherent in all organized political violence—and even when such violence is a necessary and legitimate self-defense of liberty, justice and human dignity." Apparently, the way to read Malraux's novels is to treat the historical situations in them as mere pretexts for the display of a higher conflict. "Malraux's heroes," Frank concludes, "were never simply engaged in a battle against a particular social or economic injustice; they were always somehow struggling against the limitations of life itself and the humiliations of destiny." Not only the heroes but, as noted above, the villains, too. Logically, Frank is right against Frohock: for Malraux to be too heavily committed on the side of the Loyalists is inconsistent with his claim to be dedicated to humanity in general. "The concern of the writer [Malraux]," asseverates Geoffrey H. Hartman, another contributor to Lewis's collection, "is not for one region or religion or even for the larger-scale conflict of various nations: it is for the survival of Man on earth."

As I read the pieces in *Malraux*, many of them of unusual brilliance, I kept wondering where were these critics, both the Americans and the Europeans, during the events to which Malraux's novels were a response, and what was their own response to those events? How did they react in the twenties to the mood of European decline which evoked Malraux's *Temptation of the West*? How did they feel about communism in the days when Malraux was a commissar in China and when he wrote *The Conquerors* and *Man's Fate*? How about the operation of Stalin's secret police in Loyalist Spain when Malraux organized an air squadron, raised money in the United States for hospital equipment to be turned over to the Stalinist-controlled government, and composed *Man's Hope*? Logically, Professor Frank was right, but in fact *Man's Hope* was the apologetic composition of an agent. And what did the critics think about the left vanguardists' combat against Nazism portrayed in *Days of Wrath,* and about Malraux's abandonment of revolution and his service in the French

Resistance during the war? Do they see any connection between his turn to De Gaulle's nationalist Europeanism and his postwar immersion in global art history?

There is nothing in *Malraux* to indicate that any of its contributors (with exceptions noted) ever shared Malraux's passionate need to act. Aesthetically perceptive, and engaging in speculation on a high level, these pieces are manuscripts found in a bottle—as if their authors had been living in another century than the one which Malraux has been agitating with such fervor. They apprehend the drama in his writings but not his writings in the drama of the time. Yet in the periods when the novels were written, most of these critics probably did react, at least intellectually, to the historical challenge. Was their reaction the same as Malraux's? Was their conception of the human situation also such that, like him, they would have collaborated in suppressing facts about the Communist Party for the sake of its potential service to man? If they are not in accord with Malraux on these great matters why be silent about it? Has detachment from current history become part of the "discipline" of literary criticism? Perhaps Professor Lewis's collection exemplifies the moratorium on political thinking which has prevailed in criticism since the war. If such be the case, Malraux is an author admirably suited to bring out the weakness of criticism cleansed of historical concreteness.

In the articles quoted, analysis of Malraux's specific meanings tends to be swallowed up in explications of his profundity. In contrast, two other contributors to *Malraux*, Nicola Chiaramonte and Claude-Edmonde Magny, are opposed to Malraux's outlook and his vision of history; they find his reasoning cloudy and his experience lacking in wholeness. Yet the attack of these critics also takes place in the arena of man's ultimate situation. They reject Malraux's philosophy but do not doubt that the issue is philosophical. For Chiaramonte, Malraux is possessed by "the demons of action," who distract him from the norms of the classical tradition to which he aspires—a conclusion which is probably applicable to the majority of modern artists and which, in this instance, is a Dostoyevskian reflection on Malraux's reflection of Dostoyevsky. Magny, repelled by Malraux's obsession with the separateness of human beings and their inability to communicate with one another, finds in him a fatal error, rather than a characteristic way of distorting contemporary realities. "As for estheticism," concludes Chiaramonte, extending Malraux's metaphysical drama into his art theory, "Malraux is an esthete in the sense that art is for him the only realm in which man can meet fate on equal terms." Together and separately, the criticisms in *Malraux* are variations on the theme of Blanchot: Malraux is interested in art (or revolution, God, History, evil, heroism, action, archeology, Europe), but he is above all interested in Man. Doubts concerning his politics, his literary sensibility, the generosity of his feelings, his intellectual clarity are drowned in this leitmotif.

It is symptomatic that though Malraux is a voluminous author, the same passages are chosen by critic after critic to illustrate the wide span of his thought. Many find the following, from Malraux's early *Temptation of the West,* laden with significance: "For you, absolute reality was first God then man; but *man is dead,* following God, and in anguish you are seeking someone to whom to entrust his strange legacy" (italics in original). Another favorite, from Malraux's last novel, *The Walnut Trees of Altenburg,* is Dietrich Berger's remark before killing himself: "Well, you know, *whatever happens,* if I had to live another life, I should want none other than Dietrich Berger's" (italics in original). This repetition of tag statements helps

to transmute Malraux's writings into a philosophical cor-
relative of themselves.

Some of Malraux's commentators cling more persistently
to his abiding truths than does Malraux himself. Writing
some time ago to contributor Armand Hoog, Malraux confessed that "little of what I dramatized in *La Condition
Humaine* holds true." This rare token of modesty from the
moneylender of the absolute is immediately rejected by
Professor Hoog. "But the central problem of the novel," he
protests, "has outlived a once significant historico-political
conjuncture." For Hoog the Chinese Revolution and all
that it holds for the future of mankind represents a passing
"conjuncture" that has lost its meaning, while Malraux's
literary "problem," even though based on an erroneous estimate of the facts, is still worth talking about. In elevating
the issue presented in *Man's Fate,* that is to say, its conclusions about the human situation, above the actual history of
mankind, Hoog typifies the approach to Malraux we have
been discussing in that it sees everything in reverse. Instead
of analyzing Malraux's pattern of ideas in terms of the "historico-political conjunctures" of the 1920's and 1930's by
which they were shaped, these critics treat historical conflicts as secondary ingredients in a literature existing for its
own sake.

William Righter's *The Rhetorical Hero* also sees things
in reverse. If it is appropriate to think of Malraux as a
hero, I should say that he is not a hero made out of words
but that he is a courageous man whose words and ideas get
in the way of his knowing what he is doing. A work of great
analytical dexterity, *The Rhetorical Hero* follows a curious
design: evoking Malraux as an heroic figure of our century
of crisis, one whom De Gaulle saluted with, *"Enfin, un
homme!"* and Drieu La Rochelle hailed as "the new man,"
it empties this image by exposing Malraux's bombast, his

"meretricious dazzle," obscurantism, idea juggling, intellectual arrogance. Yet Righter manages to turn each defect of his hero in the direction of a philosophical virtue—or, when this is not possible, to tuck it out of sight under other defects. Malraux is damaged as a writer, thinker, public personality, but kept intact as a poetic monument of the age. By the critic's willful disregard of moral or political values, the author is insulated, as if magically, against shortcomings that are fatal to both writers and heroes. "Action, creation, expression," says Righter about Malraux's *Museum without Walls,* "are dissolved into one another, caught up in the Museum's dialectic of involvement and detachment, often frozen together in the same rhetorical cliché, or carried by the same rhetorical élan." This is an elaborate way of saying that Malraux's art history relies on verbal excitement to blow up platitudes into cosmic confrontations. My own reaction to Malraux on art was largely in accord with this view. But Righter stubbornly refuses to enter his judgment as final: it is but a phase of his exposition of Malraux's metaphysical "tragedy." Malraux, Righter concludes, may be a hero chiefly in the realm of words, but this realm is a grand and enduring one where "the problems of man and creation, action and contemplation, have their genuine if shadowy existence."

In sum, the problem in current criticism of Malraux is not lack of awareness of his qualities, but a persistent tendency to falsify the scale of his achievement through stringing his writings upon the lofty scaffolding of the issue of human destiny. To take a decisive instance: Righter points out that "in the novels the model situation is that of the single individual faced by the extreme demands of the historical moment." This means that to grasp the drama of the novels we must understand the nature of the historical events with which they deal. Well, what are (or were) these "extreme demands" in the specific "moments" dealt with by Malraux? Malraux's conception of them will determine whether his characters' suffering was the effect of tragic necessity or of their author's intellectual confusion. In both China and Spain, Malraux was convinced that history decreed that whatever the individual's disagreements with communism he was obliged to join in the action on the side of Communists. For Malraux the individual is an actor in history, but history is organized by totalitarian professionals. Holding back from membership in the Party, Malraux was a fellow traveler who reserved the privilege of doubt and introspection about history itself. Like Koestler in *Darkness at Noon,* he accepted, however, a servitude to the Party no less paralyzing intellectually than membership: belief in the identity of the Party and history, the very mystique which caused the old Bolsheviks to sacrifice themselves upon the altar of Party loyalty and which even Trotsky took some years to shake off. This belief determines the content of Malraux's "model situation" and his view of human destiny, heroism, etc. What the historical moment demands of the individual is what the Party demands. The Party may be wrong as to what men are to think, feel and hope for, but it cannot in Malraux's novels of the thirties be wrong about what they are to do. Chiaramonte tells how Malraux out of fear of damaging the authority of the International refused during the Moscow Trials to respond to a request by Trotsky that he confirm a fact regarding a meeting with him. The historical situation in which the individual acts has been defined by the Party line; faced by it he can only play his part, heroically or otherwise. If he is destroyed, he is a victim of fate. In *The Conquerors, Man's Fate, Man's Hope,* the action of the individual takes place within a larger action whose course and rhythm are predetermined. As the story opens, the "great action" of history is already under way—the protagonist cannot affect its direction, he can only "tie himself" to it and share its plunge like Ahab tied to Moby Dick. ("To tie oneself to a great action of some kind," exclaimed Malraux in *The Conquerors*, "not to let go of it, to be united and intoxicated by *it*.") It is the force of an action that attracts Malraux, not the possibility that might be realized through it—the distinction between Stalin's mode of action and Lenin's meant nothing to him. The individual enters into history as into a current (Malraux's heroes are intellectuals who volunteer to "appear" in events, not people trapped in them). He acts not in the expectation of any social consequence but in order to experience maximum potency, the thrill of having a role in a conflict that will be long remembered, and the romance of identifying himself either with the power of the rulers or with the sufferings of mankind. Once engaged in the plot of history, his choice is limited to the manner of his dying, though his end may prove to be an ironic effect of chance. The actor is at a remove from the event in which he acts—what Malraux calls "fate" is the rigid separation of the external action (history) from its human components, a conception which, oddly, none of the critics under discussion has thought to contrast with fate as it works in Greek drama *through reversal of the hero's own action*. In the final analysis, the Spanish Civil War is as "gratuitous" to Malraux's volunteers as is a murder to Gide's Lafcadio. In Malraux, absolute determinism brings about a state of unreality identical to that produced by absolute whim; and the two combine in Malraux's scanning of world art.

It is within the dramatic system of politically predetermined events that Malraux's grimly resigned activist dandies, their necks outstretched for the blows of necessity and chance, ruminate on the human condition. Contrasted with the noble (or vile) agent-victims of history are the stinkers, those who save their skin or their conscience by sneaking out of "the moment" and its demands. The setting is a fictional equivalent of the Bolshevik universe, in which humanity is divided into an elite of violence locked in a war unto death and a mob of individualist defectors condemned to oblivion. Like thousands of intellectuals in the thirties, Malraux took the Communists' word that the Party was the maker of history and that to oppose it meant turning one's back on human dignity and hope. When, at the time of the Stalin-Hitler Pact, Malraux broke with communism he repudiated history too; that is to say, he continued to identify the Party with history, but in a negative way, so that together with other ex-Communists and fellow travelers he gave up both in order to seek in art a beyond-historical system of individual acts of creation.

For Malraux, then, the human situation is constituted by action under modern totalitarian conditions. One need only reject this idea of the Party as history-maker and an entirely different conception of the individual's part in history emerges—that is to say, "the" human situation turns into something entirely different. There are, no doubt, situations (wars, insurrections, exiles) in which the grip of history is relentless; but to those caught in them they are nightmares rather than, as to Malraux, opportunities for grandeur and for relief from the pettiness of daily life. And though collective catastrophes may be inescapable, even in them the individual may have a say as to how the event shall turn out, as well as to what it requires of him. His part is not limited to courage, resignation and pathos. Also, on the stage of expanded individual possibility, leadership has a less absolute role; the chance that the general staff of his Party has wrongly estimated the "extreme demands of the historical moment" becomes a paramount concern of every conscious political actor. What may be most needed is not heroically to follow the Party (any party) into the abyss but, on the contrary, to resist the Party, to expose its delusions, even to fight to supplant it.

That Malraux's "model situation" basically misrepresents both the power of the individual and the nature of the historical moment is demonstrated by the attitude he took toward Trotsky. In his view, the former commander of the Red Army in refusing to submit to the Party's dictation had removed himself from history (during the Spanish Civil War that other, less mannerly, poet of death and destiny, Hemingway, was to refer sneeringly to intellectuals [Trotsky] who sat safely in Mexico dictating criticisms, while men and women bled to death in the streets of Madrid). It did not occur to Malraux that Trotsky's attack on the policies of the Communist International was itself an action, one whose effects have been beyond calculation. Nor could Malraux have understood Kierkegaard's observation that "in Greece philosophizing was a mode of action."

After a glimpse of the specific content of Malraux's notions of fate, action and history, it seems obvious that criticism of Malraux ought to begin by dismantling his verbal screen of "the human condition" in order to get at what is actually reflected in his texts. Yet neither Righter nor the contributors to *Malraux* has anything significant to say about the part of Malraux's politics in determining for him the nature of the confrontation between the individual and history—though Chiaramonte does outline with great precision Malraux's complex relations with the Communist Party. Description of the action of the novels remains suspended, as Malraux wished the action to be, in generalizations. Malraux's pretension to be writing about Man in History is accepted without hesitation. "The fact of cruelty or indifference," says Righter, "or of a particular death may put all human qualities in question." Perhaps. The trouble is that the death of Kyo in *Man's Fate* does no such thing; it puts in question the decisions in Moscow that brought him to his death and the cause for which he died. Above all, it puts in question Malraux's severance of action from criticism, in short, his entire approach to the individual who is faced by the need to act politically.

We have said that in Malraux's novels the characters find themselves engaged in actions already in progress and which they cannot affect. The ready-made event calls for the ready-made actor—the formula of melodrama. In Malraux the "great act" of history is enacted by a cast of melodramatic types with the whole of humanity for their audience. Indeed, consciousness of this audience is an essential motive in their performance as men of destiny. Since Lenin in his workingman's cap, the Bolsheviks have been men in costume and players to the crowd. In Malraux's thinking, action constantly blends into acting: with historical script in hand, the only problem is which part to play and how to play it.

When I read Malraux's novels in the thirties they were for me "first of all" thrillers, complete with settings in movie chiaroscuro, Dostoyevskian assassins and decadents, mood music of the Furies and of the spheres. That one could not in *Man's Fate* or *Days of Wrath* shake off the impression of *déjà vu* made these novels perhaps more mysterious in that their plots revolved about the vanguard issue of the Bolshevik Revolution. Like "modernizations" in reverse, Malraux's fictions reproduced the action of the twentieth century with old stage sets and a nineteenth-century cast of characters—a remodeled Raskolnikov, Svidrigailov, Kirillov. It is precisely the presence of these familiar personages that accounts for the enthusiasm aroused by the novels in conservative readers who would have been appalled by a naked confrontation with Malraux's adventuristic politics. Another baffling feature was the irrelevance of the tense theorizing that occupied so much of the dialogue and introspection. The total effect, as in movie melodrama generally, was to create a sense of estrangement or unreality about everyday happenings.

I find these impressions reinforced by Righter and the critics in *Malraux*, though their observations fail to shake their convictions that they are dealing with tragedy on the grand scale. Several call attention to Malraux's "cinematographic" methods of composition, not only in the novels but in his art history. His specialty is the close-up: Tchen with his dagger poised to strike his sleeping victim through the mosquito netting; the shadow of the doomed Katov projected by the train's headlight against the white wall. "What is left to us," comments Righter on the *Museum without Walls*, "is the staring face, the curious curve of a torso, the puzzling but eloquent design. Something in their isolation helps convey that sense of 'deeper life' that Malraux is seeking." Magny lists Malraux's "opiates": the Universe, Music, Charity, Night—"the vast sleepy silence of the Chinese night, with its smell of camphor and of leaves, extended all the way to the Pacific, enveloped the night outside time: not a ship call, not a rifle shot . . ." The irrelevance of the dialogue to the action except to generate atmosphere is less frequently noted, perhaps because the critic's labor has supplied connections lacking in the direct response of sensibility. Chiaramonte, however, has shrewdly spotted the "strange gap between Kyo's interrupted political argument and his sudden communion with the age-old sorrow of man." And Righter, that all-perceiving and strangely permissive Righter, shows how the aesthetic and historical analogies that constitute Malraux's art history are based on broken theoretical bridges and massive name-dropping, like Great Artists mentioned in a movie or Sunday supplement article. "Almost chosen at random a single paragraph may contain the names: Renoir, Chartres, Giotto, Rheims, Bamberg, Naumberg, Senlis, Mantes, Laon, Goya, Bayeux, Manet, Michelangelo, Donatello, Rembrandt, Lastmann, Elsheimer, El Greco, Bassano, Piero della Francesca—and several of them repeated."

That the melodrama of Malraux's fiction is carried over into his art history is not without its good effects, since the History-Consciousness of modern art needs to be announced with gongs. After almost fifty years of Picasso, Brancusi, Modigliani, it is apparently still necessary to call attention to the activity of twentieth-century paintings and sculpture in resurrecting the art of other epochs on a global basis, and Malraux, with his archeological background and his worry over the decline of Europe, has done so with maximum emphasis.

In his art criticism Malraux returned to his starting point, the decline of the West. Taking the position that modern art represents a break with the past and a recapitulation of it under new psychic conditions, Malraux has had many pertinent things to say about the art of the past one hundred years, though little that had not been said earlier and with less pomp.

The trouble, as in his novels, lies in his corny idea of the great role. Malraux will have nothing to do with anyone less than a god or a hero—and the god must be dying and the hero hopeless. The art act, like the act of his political heroes, begins in a system of existing acts to which the living artist ties himself. As in the novels, the "great act" (now the Masterpiece) separates itself from the time and place of its enactment and communes across the centuries with other world-shaping performances. There is no room in

Malraux's art theory for the unceasing creation that every-where manifests itself in visual and oral language and which is the ground for the creation of masterpieces, just as there was no room in his theory of the human situation for the social and economic development which is the ground for victory in political revolution.

Also as in the novels, the situation of modern man as artist is predetermined: for *him* there will be no creation of masterpieces. For Malraux, the outstanding characteristic of the painting and sculpture of our time is its extinction of content. The end of art has come: there is nothing left but to build the Imaginary Museum—as with Spengler the end of the West had come and there was nothing left but to absorb its cultural creations into a system of analogies. Transmuting the art of the past into metaphors, the historian becomes the rival of the artist. While the latter re-creates the empty forms of the paintings of earlier centuries, Malraux accumulates through the juxtaposition of words and reproductions the essence of art in all times and places. The global curator, a species of spiritual bureaucrat, takes over from "the doomed painter" and emerges as the master creator of the age.

In claiming that modern art is empty of content Malraux had in mind religious content, gods with traditional attributes. But he had also fallen victim to a cliché of academic art criticism and had mistaken a "moment" in modern art—analytical Cubism—for the development of abstract art as a whole. But what above all blinds him to new content (he sees Pollock as a variation on Masson and Fautrier) is once again his acceptance of an absolute historical determinism, now cultural rather than political, and his tacit denial of the capacity of individuals to generate new possibilities through their action. In art, as formerly in politics, he restricts the power of the single person to the heroic nuance. No wonder ĥe dares to present art history as consisting of fantastic juxtapositions of African masks, Russian folktale illustrations, Buddhist frescoes, drawings by madmen—you can't dispute a nuance any more than you can De Gaulle's *"Enfin un homme!"*

The all-too-often-repeated notion that the crisis of art in our time is owing to the death of the gods is only half an idea. Granted that the history of art is largely a history of idol-making, it is also a history of insights into the nature of things, and a history of feelings, of responses to color and texture, of manual skills. The modern break with the past owes more to science, the machine, social upheaval and introspection than it does to a declining devotion to inherited other worlds of the imagination. Our problem is less that the skies are empty than that our minds are mystified by the flood of new knowledge and new powers in the midst of the old restraints. To this mystification Malraux's writings have provided a swelling echo. The task of criticism is not to echo the echo, but to contract it to the scale of the real world.

9

Guilt to the
Vanishing Point

"In this harsh world draw
thy breath in pain to tell my story," the dying Hamlet
begged his friend Horatio. Telling can, apparently, require a sacrifice—in Hamlet's view, the supreme sacrifice
of remaining alive. Then why tell it? What good will it do?
It is a shocking story; to repeat it can only induce bad
dreams, particularly in the few survivors of the bloody
tragedy. Also, the story is confused and points to no edifying conclusion. For Horatio to accede to Hamlet's appeal,
the passion of the friend and the poet must overcome the
impulse of the man to seek relief from the past in oblivion.

Human beings, it is generally assumed, are entitled to
peace of mind, and this privilege ought to be surrendered
only if it can be demonstrated that the painful recalling of
miseries will serve some useful purpose—that of teaching a
moral lesson, or providing social therapy, or stimulating
patriotism, or promoting progress. Thus press reports of
testimony in the trial of "The Attorney General versus
Adolf, the son of Adolf Karl Eichmann" concluded their
horrid accounts by arguing apologetically that virtuous

ends might be served: "It is hoped," ran the refrain, "that bringing these evils to light will prevent anything like them from ever happening again." Dr. Servatius, chief attorney for the defense, asked in his summation that the judges decide the case in such a way as to "serve as a warning signpost for history" and a contribution to the cause of peace.

But suppose the justification for the telling were inadequate or even absurd? Could one really believe that the trial of Eichmann would deter mass murderers in the future, or that it would advance international relations? Suppose the only predictable result of recalling the shootings, hangings and gassings was to arouse fright in susceptible imaginations' and to perpetuate in Jews the memory of injuries suffered? To weigh the narration of Germany's "Final Solution of the Jewish Problem" in terms of its probable effects was all but to argue for its suppression. And it is a fact that prominent among those who condemned in advance the proceedings in Jerusalem were liberals representing ideals of mental health and social amelioration. Even among the supporters of the trial, who dared squarely to represent the dead? Who dared to assert that the story of their sufferings must be recounted regardless of consequences? Yet is not the right of the victim to have his story told an *absolute* right?

The Eichmann Trial undertook the function of tragic poetry, that of making the pathetic and terrifying past live again in the mind. But it had to carry out this function on a world stage ruled by the utilitarian code. One read in the press immediately after Eichmann's capture that, despite international law, he was to be tried in Israel in order to satisfy popular passion there, particularly among the ex-Europeans whose familes had perished in the murder program. This was held to be objectionable. In a culture conditioned by psychiatry to interpret actions as "outlets" of feeling, the excitement in Israel over the trapped Nazi raised the spectre of pathological fixation, vendetta, blood lust. What were the enraged Israelis going to do to Eichmann to avenge themselves for the Jewish blood shed by the Nazis? Sermons and warnings poured from partisans of forgiveness, legality and scientific objectivity (as if to forgive or be "objective" about someone who'd murdered one's wife and children in cold blood were not a thousand times as sick as to avenge oneself). With the liberal world demanding, "State the purpose of the trial or convict yourselves of Nazi-like barbarism," Ben-Gurion replied that revenge was out of the question and that the purpose of the trial was to alert mankind to the dangers of anti-Semitism. Others suggested that the trial aimed at stimulating Israeli patriotism by reminding the new generation that while their fathers could go to their deaths unresisting in a despairing failure of will, they, through national independence, had gained the spirit and the means to fight back. With statements like these in mind, Dr. Servatius was able at the end of the trial to characterize it as a "political case."

Yet all these useful and forward-looking motives, not free of false notes, were but a disguise of reasonableness for the irresistible demand for a tragic retelling—the demand of multitudes of Jews who had been inconceivably brought into a psychic unity like that of an antique folk by an inconceivable assault, their not-to-be-denied poetic passion to hear related, and before the whole of humanity, the terrible fate of their stricken relatives and ancestors. The trial was a way of giving public shape to a tormenting memory that each had kept underground.

But the need forced upon Israel to justify the trial in terms of its moral and historical effects was bound to lead to distortions, as is always the case when a moral "message" is imposed upon a tragic drama. It is some of these distortions that I shall discuss here, with the understanding that I intend no criticism of any of the officials concerned in the case—for not only were they under the outside pressure to have the trial "make sense" but they were obliged also, as we shall see, to participate in incongruities by the legal situation itself.

Had the Eichmann Trial been "a political case," or *only* a political case, it should have been conducted quite differently. Compared, for example, with other show trials of our time, such as the Moscow Trials or the Hiss Case, the prosecution of Eichmann shows few signs of belonging to the same species. In those cases, the political message was *the* point, and every bit of evidence concerning the guilt of the defendant was organized to hammer that message home. Different as were the procedures of the Soviet People's Courts from those of courts ruled by the Bill of Rights, the offenses charged in each were presented in such a way as to appear less important in themselves than as symbols of menacing conspiracies carried on by thousands of active, shadowy culprits not present in the courtroom. The trial in each of these cases was a cautionary parable hitting at those hidden enemies prepared to do damage unless the law prevented them. Since the Moscow defendants and Hiss represented a general menace, it was not necessary that the individual misconduct alleged should be established with the same gravity regarding the facts as in an ordinary crime. Thus the Russians visibly fabricated fables out of police-inspired "confessions"; while our own federal prosecutor, overleaping the Statute of Limitations in order to reach into a previous decade, won a verdict of *perjury* by presenting proof of *espionage* in the form of old typewriters, Persian rugs, prothonotary warblers, pumpkins, and other fanciful cuttings from the world between every-day life and mystery literature.

In Jerusalem, by contrast, there was no present danger, at least not from this defendant or his like. All the dreadful deeds had been done; and experiencing the actual past was everything, beyond any lesson. Thus masses of data were piled into the record for no other reason than that there were people to recount them. Once the testimony concerning the anguish of the Jews began, all formal restraints, whether required for legally upholding an indictment or for setting "a signpost for history," became obstacles in the way of the narrative impulse. Everyone with a personal or group tragedy to relate had to be given his day in court as in some vast collective dirge. For almost two months, the defendant and the world heard from individuals escaped from the grave about fathers and mothers, gray-beards, adolescents, babies, starved, beaten to death, strangled, machine-gunned, gassed, burned. One who had been a boy in Auschwitz had to tell how children had been selected by height for the gas chambers. The gruesome humor of the Nazis was not forgotten—the gas chamber with a sign on it with the name of a Jewish foundation and bearing a copper Star of David—nor the gratuitous sadism of SS officers. Public relations strategists everywhere, both amateurs and professionals, watching the reaction of the German press, the liberal press, the lunatic-fringe press, listening to their neighbors, studying interviews with men and women on the street, cried out, Too much, too much, the mind of the audience is becoming dulled in these hot afternoons, the horrors are losing their capacity to shock, the trial should be brought to an end. And still another witness, one who had saved himself by crawling out from under a heap of corpses after he had been shot and left for dead, had to tell how the victims had been forced to lay themselves head to foot one on top of the other in order to be murdered conveniently. . . .

Most of this testimony may have been legally admissible as bearing on the *corpus delicti* of the total Nazi crime but seemed subject to question when not tied to the part in it of the defendant's Department of Jewish Affairs. Counsel for the defense, however, shrewdly allowing himself to be swept by the current of dreadful recollections, rarely raised an objection. Would not the emotional catharsis eventually brought on by this awfulness have a calming, if not exhausting, effect likely to improve his client's chances? Those who feared "emotionalism" at the trial showed less understanding than Dr. Servatius of the route by which man achieves the distance necessary for fairness toward enemies. Interruptions came largely from the bench, which numerous times rebuked the Attorney General for letting his witnesses run on, though it, too, made no serious effort to choke off the flow.

But there was a contrast even more decisive than a hunger for fact between the trial in Jerusalem and those in Moscow and New York. In the two last, the trials *marked the beginning of a new course.* The Moscow Trials led to the liquidation of the old Bolsheviks and the tightening of Stalin's dictatorship. The Hiss Case initiated the period of militant anti-communism, with repentant ex-Communists in the vanguard of purges of government agencies and investigations of institutions and individuals. These trials were properly termed "political cases" in that the trial itself was a political act producing political consequences. But what could the Eichmann Trial initiate? Of what new course could it mark the beginning? The Eichmann Case looked to the past, not to the future. It was the conclusion of the first phase of a process of tragic recollection, and of refining that recollection, that will last as long as there are

Jews. As such, it was beyond politics and had no need of justification by a "message."

"It is not an individual that is in the dock at this historical trial—" said Ben-Gurion, "and not the Nazi regime alone—but anti-Semitism throughout history." How could supplying Eichmann with a platform on which to maintain that one could collaborate in the murder of millions of Jews *without being an anti-Semite* contribute to a verdict against anti-Semitism? And if it was not an individual who was in the dock, why was the trial, as we shall observe later, all but scuttled in the attempt to prove Eichmann a "fiend"? These questions touch the root of confusion in the prosecution's case.

It might be contended, of course, that Eichmann in stubbornly denying anti-Semitic feelings was lying or insisting on a private definition of anti-Semitism. But in either event he was the wrong man for the kind of case outlined by Ben-Gurion and set forth in the indictment. In such a case the defendant should serve as a clear example and no arguments should be needed to make him represent the issue. One who could be linked to anti-Semitism only by overcoming his denials of it is scarcely a good specimen of the Jew-baiter throughout the ages, who is proud of his hatred and feels superior because of it. Shout at Eichmann though he might, the prosecutor could not establish that the defendant was falsifying how he felt about Jews or that what he did feel fell into the generally recognized category of anti-Semitism. Yes, he believed that the Jews were "enemies of the Reich," and such a belief is, of course, typical of "patriotic" anti-Semites; but he believed in the Jew-as-enemy in a kind of abstract, theological way, like a member of a cult speculating on the nature of things. The real question was how one passed from anti-Semitism of this theoretical sort to murder, and the answer to this question is not to be found in anti-Semitism itself. In regard to Eichmann the murder motive was to be found in the Nazi outlook, which contained a principle separate from and far worse than anti-Semitism, a principle so poisonous that it could make the poison of anti-Semitism itself more virulent. Under the guidance of this Nazi principle one might, as Eichmann contended, feel personally friendly toward the Jews and still be their murderer. Not through fear of disobeying orders, as Eichmann kept trying to explain, but through a systematically induced megalomania that made non-Nazis appear first as inferior creatures, then as mere things or even nothings. This infusion of limitless self-adoration (not of the individual self but of the self in Party uniform) produced a peculiar giddiness that began with half-acceptance of the vicious absurdities contained in the Nazi interpretation of history and grew with each of Hitler's victories into a permanent lightheadedness and a sense of magical rightness that was able to respond to any proposal, and the more outrageous the better, with "Why not, let's do it . . ." At any rate, the substance of Eichmann's testimony was that all his actions flowed directly from his membership in the Party and the SS, and though the prosecutor did his utmost to prove actual personal hatred of Jews his success on this score was doubtful and the anti-Semitic "lesson" weakened to that extent.

But if the trial failed to expose the special Nazi mania so deadly to Jews, as well as to anyone else upon whom it happened to light (e.g., the Gypsies), neither did it warn very effectively against the ordinary anti-Semitism of which the Nazis made such effective use in Germany and wherever else they could find it. If anti-Semitism was on trial in Jerusalem, why was it not identified, and with enough emphasis to capture the notice of the world press, as an instrument of

Eichmann's Department of Jewish Affairs, as exemplified by the betrayal and murder of Jews by non-police and non-Party anti-Semites in Germany, as well as in Poland, Russia, Czechoslovakia, Hungary? The infamous Wansee Conference, called by Heydrich in January, 1942 to organize the material and technical means to put to death the eleven million Jews spread throughout the nations of Europe, was attended by representatives of major organs of the German state, including the Reich Minister of the Interior, the State Secretary in charge of the Four Year Plan, the Reich Minister of Justice, the Under Secretary of Foreign Affairs. The measures for annihilation proposed and accepted at the conference affected industry, transportation, civilian agencies of government. Heydrich, in opening the conference, followed the reasoning and even the phraseology of the order issued earlier by Goering, which authorized the Final Solution as "a complement to" previous "solutions" for eliminating the Jews from German living space through violence, economic strangulation, forced emigration and evacuation. In other words, the promulgators of the murder plan made clear that physically exterminating the Jews of Europe was but an extension of the anti-Semitic measures already operating in every phase of German life, and that the new conspiracy counted on the assumption that the general anti-Semitism that had made those measures effective could be sharpened into a readiness for murder. This, in fact, turned out to be the case. Since the magnitude of the plan made secrecy impossible, once the wheels had begun to turn, persons controlling German industries, social institutions, and armed forces became, through their anti-Semitism or their tolerance of it, conscious accomplices of Hitler's crimes; whether murderers in the first degree or in a lesser one was a matter to be determined individually.

What more could be asked for a trial intended to warn the world against anti-Semitism than this opportunity to expose the exact link between the respectable anti-Semite and the concentration camp brute? Not in Eichmann's cloudy anti-Semitism but in the common anti-Semitism of the sober German functionary and man of affairs lay the potential warning of the trial. No doubt many of the citizens of the Third Reich had conceived their anti-Semitism as an "innocent" dislike of Jews, as do others like them today. The Final Solution proved that the Jew-baiter of any variety exposes himself to being implicated in the criminality and madness of others. Ought not an edifying trial to have made every effort to demonstrate this once and for all by showing how representative types of "mere" anti-Semites were drawn step by step into the program of skull-bashings and gassings? The prosecutor in his opening remarks did refer to "the germ of anti-Semitism" among the Germans, which Hitler "stimulated and transformed." But if there was evidence at the trial that aimed over Eichmann's head at his collaborators in the societies where he functioned, the press seems to have missed it.

Nor did the trial devote much attention to exposing the usefulness of anti-Semitism to the Nazis, both in building their own power and in destroying that of rival organizations and states. Certainly, one of the best ways of warning the world against anti-Semitism is to demonstrate how it works as a dangerous weapon in disintegrating, or capturing control of, social institutions. Eichmann himself is a model of how the myth of the enemy-Jew can be used to transform the ordinary man of present-day society into a menace to *all* his neighbors. Do patriots everywhere know enough about how the persecution of the Jews in Germany and later in the occupied countries contributed to terrorizing the populations, splitting apart individuals and groups, arousing the meanest and most dishonest impulses, pulverizing trust and personal dignity, and finally forcing people to follow their masteɩs into the abyss by making them partners in unspeakable crimes? The career of Eichmann made the trial a potential showcase for anti-Semitic demoralization: fearful of being mistaken for a Jew he seeks protection in his Nazi uniform; clinging to the enemy-Jew idea he is forced to overcome habits of politeness and neighborliness; once in power, he begins to give vent to a criminal opportunism that causes him to alternate between megalomania and envy of those above him. "Is this the type of citizen you want?" the trial should have asked the nations of the world. But though such a characterization of the "little man" corrupted by anti-Semitism would in no way have diminished Eichmann's guilt, the prosecutor, more deeply involved in the tactics of a criminal case than a political one, would have none of it.

Finally, if the mission of the trial was to convict anti-Semitism, how could it have failed to post before the world the contrasting fates of the countries in which the Final Solution was aided by native Jew-haters—i.e., Germany, Poland, Hungary, Czechoslovakia—and those in which it met the obstacle of human solidarity—Denmark, Holland, Italy, Bulgaria, France? Should not everyone have been awakened to the fact, as an outstanding phenomenon of our time, that the nations poisoned by anti-Semitism proved less fortunate in regard to their own freedom than those whose citizens showed the inclination to save their Jewish compatriots from the transports? Wasn't this meaning of Eichmann's experience in various countries worth highlighting?

As the first collective confrontation of the Nazi outrage, the trial of Eichmann represented a recovery of the Jews from the shock of the death camps, a recovery that took fifteen years and which is still by no means complete (though it would be an error to believe that it could be hastened by silence). Only across a softening distance of time could the epic accounting begin. It is already difficult to recall how little was known before the trial of what had been done to the Jews of Europe. It is not that the facts of the persecution were unavailable; most of the information elicited in Jerusalem had been brought to the surface by the numerous War Crimes tribunals and investigating commissions, and by reports, memoirs and survivors' accounts. As early as 1952, Gerald Reitlinger's *The Final Solution* had organized into sequence the various phases of the extermination program and the horrors visited upon different groups of victims. Yet it is questionable that much of this growing body of knowledge entered the general consciousness, or even that of many Jews. Even today the Nazi conspiracy is rarely grasped in the various stages and objectives through which it developed as the Party leaders reacted to world events and tested how far the conscience of civilization would allow itself to be outraged. For most who lived through this period, the Nuremberg Laws, asphyxiation buses, rabbis scrubbing pavements, boycotts, death marches, the Crystal Night atrocities, gas chambers are all jumbled together in a vague hurt as of a bruise received in the dark. One still meets people who speak of six million *German* Jews killed. Perhaps no crime in history has been better documented or more vaguely apprehended.

One reason for our ignorance lies in the character and interests of our "communications" media, a subject we cannot enter into here. Another reason lies within ourselves, in the nature of our ideas and of our way of understanding large public occurrences. The scientific temper of our time has so accustomed us to generalize about "forces," "trends" and "processes" that we pay little attention to the events themselves, has so accustomed us to look behind the happening for its impersonal causes that we give scant notice to the human actors engaged in the doing. The deadliest foe is dissolved into an abstraction; he becomes an instance or a symptom.

But the unfolding of a crime cannot be grasped except through the actions of the perpetrator of the crime. Without Iago, the tragedy of Othello disintegrates into a dream of jealousy. In the absence of the Nazi enemy whose complex system of assaults was in fact a single continuing attack, the tragedy of the Jews lacked coherence as well as particularity—those shot on the Polish border, gassed at Belsen, seemed, as Dr. Servatius was to suggest they were, but another category of war victims. The ordeal of the Jews was fully exposed with the opening of the death camps, but to absorb this knowledge into experience it was necessary to confront the image of the assassin and the motive and method of his attack. Only the presence of the enemy could bring all these disparate acts into focus as a violent thrust against the Jews in particular which they in particular were compelled to endure and resist.

One knew, of course, that the ones most directly responsible were Hitler, Himmler, Goering, Heydrich. But when one tried to fix these figures at the center of the anti-Jewish fury, they failed somehow to stay in place, less perhaps because they were already dead by the time the entire scale of their deed had risen to view than because killing Jews was only a fraction of their crimes; carried back to the masters of the Reich, the sufferings of the Jews blended with those of the Czechs, the Poles, the Russians, indeed masses of injured throughout the world.

With the seizure of Eichmann there appeared suddenly a living protagonist for *this* crime, a man bound to the misery of the Jews as his specialty, his sole reason for being. The chief of the Department of Jewish Affairs, Sec. IV B4 of the combined Gestapo and SS, was particularly and totally identified with the murder plan in that he had no other role, no status or stature apart from this single function, that of ferrying Jews to their deaths. Even his comparatively low rank, of which he tried to make so much at his trial as proving his lack of authority to initiate or avoid decisions, stood as a mark of his complete association with the Jews, in that it reflected the Nazis' contempt for them— it was appropriate in their view to put the power of life and death over Jews into the hands of a mere lieutenant colonel. With Eichmann in his cage in Jerusalem it was possible for the first time to visualize the massacres that had taken place across the face of Eastern Europe not as disconnected atrocities, like outbursts of violence in an insane asylum, but as a planned and centralized undertaking aimed at the annihilation of all Jews.* By his presence, Eichmann removed the crime from the madhouse and situated it in history. Unlike other pogroms, the German atrocity now became part of the chronicle of a great nation, memorable to its members as well as to the Jews as part of their past.

The trial was thus a reenactment of the transports and the camps that brought face to face the main characters of the tragedy. As a medium of dramatic narration, however, a court trial has basic shortcomings. These were exagger-

* One wonders how many American Jews are even yet aware that "The Final Solution of the Jewish Problem," which was put into effect after the Nazis had overrun much of Europe and established puppet alliances in both the West and the East, was intended to be applied throughout the world as the Nazi victory was extended. Had the United States lost the war, which it had entered a month before Wansee, there can be no doubt that Obersturmbannführer Eichmann would have shown up in Washington to negotiate our removal to the camps.

ated in the unprecedented case of the six million. Characteristics of the judicial form hampered the public telling of the story of the Jews, at the same time that they favored the strategy of the defendant in reducing his culpability to the vanishing point.

The question-and-answer form of the examination of witnesses breaks into fragments the events described by them. In the Eichmann Case, witnesses were allowed to speak with a minimum of interruption from counsel. But as against this advantage, no witness for the prosecution actually had more than a tiny bit to tell about the gigantic catastrophe by which he had been overtaken. Nor was any order possible in the series of testimonies by survivors out of which the shape of the whole offense was to be filled out. Moreover, of the story thus received in fragments, the press communicated still smaller fragments, indeed only the minutest samples. Thus once again the world saw a splatter of atrocities but without an active human center. For the first time more than a passing glimpse was gained of the dreadful fate that befell the Jews of Europe, and this was the great contribution of the trial. But what led to this fate, in terms both of events and of the acts of persons in various degrees responsible for it, was still left largely to conjecture.

Another handicap of court procedure is that the judge's bench, unlike the narrative of the poet or storyteller in its recapture of the specific emotional quality of the event recounted, does its best to bleach out the emotional coloration of incidents as an impediment to impartial judgment. Like other scientific approaches, the law exaggerates the *neutrality* of what is done: a witness may testify that he saw X climb a wall and enter a window, but he may not describe the terror that he felt when he realized that X intended to burglarize the apartment—which makes the activity of the burglar identical with that of a householder who has lost his key. The law all but invites an Eichmann to describe himself as a "transport officer." No doubt, there is an "objective" ingredient in the actions of men, and it is possible that sequences of actions can organize themselves apart from human intention to bring about a catastrophe. The Greek theater, which emphasized the *fatality* of disaster, compensated for this emphasis by the moral protests and outcries of the Chorus. In the Eichmann Case, the calm of judicial procedure often led to new offenses, if not outrages; and something comparable to the Greek Chorus was spontaneously brought into being in Jerusalem by survivors of the camps who sprang up in the gallery from time to time to hurl curses at the defendant seated in his block of ice—but these interrupters were hastily ejected from the courtroom to quiet the seas of rage, frustration and anguish that welled up underneath it.

While, however, order could be restored, the court had no way of rectifying the imbalance between what was being claimed by the defense and what had been done in the camps. Instead of the grief and horror appropriate to the narration of tragic happenings, the law court establishes an atmosphere of balanced discussion. A trial implies a contest; the very word "defendant" contains the thought that whatever the accusation a defense is possible. This, in a way, regularizes the offense of the accused—even if he is found guilty, it will be within a category of crime known to the law and accepted by it as possessing precedents. As a defendant, Eichmann, had, by definition, a "case."

In keeping with this legal assumption that Eichmann's guilt was a subject of debate, things were discussed that are not humanly discussable. For instance, wasn't it to the advantage of the Jews to be delivered to the gas chambers more efficiently? "It cannot be denied," the defendant testified, "that this orderliness [which Eichmann had introduced into the deportations and which speeded them up] was to some extent to the benefit of the people who were deported." Given Eichmann's admissions both before and during the trial, the reasonable examination of his behavior and motives put things in grotesque light, as if the judges, the prosecutor, the spectators, had by their mere presence agreed to cooperate with the defense in respecting its monstrous hypotheses. A kind of black humor was thus precipitated at which one could not allow oneself to laugh. At this trial, the verdict of which was doomed to be incongruous—"How punish one man for six million dead?"—every analytical statement tended to turn into a ridiculous statement and a new insult to any sentiment of human order. Taking advantage to the limit of his legal privilege of minimizing his guilt by surgically separating his segment of the action from the whole—"Killing is one thing, but transportation is something else. I had nothing to do with killing"—Eichmann barely stopped short of justifying his Gestapo vocation, while condemning the Gestapo. Since he had not personally initiated the Gestapo program, he had done no wrong in carrying it out. Here the terminology of debate produces unspeakable assumptions as if in a dialogue between people who have taken dope. Defending his delivery of the Jews to the hangman as conducted in good taste and marred by no enmity to Jews, Eichmann takes for granted his right to dispose of Jews. This established, he seeks praise by calling attention to bad ways of exercising this right, that is, those of brutes and sadists. On testimony as to his having beaten a Jewish community leader from Vienna, he excuses himself for having lost his temper and enters into a dissertation on his customary gentlemanly manners—until one almost forgets what an infinite grievance and humiliation it is that any Jew, just because he was a Jew, should have had to come hat in hand to this stinking nonentity, or even been forced to talk to him. But if for the hunter of women and babies to describe himself, and be described by a respected lawyer, as merely "arranging timetables" is an insane contention, the insanity is not in Eichmann but in the logic of normal trial procedure when applied to such a case.

The necessary intellectual coolness of a courtroom favored Eichmann—I even venture to propose that counting in advance on the neutral style of the law (duplicated in that creation of law, bureaucracy) contributed to the formation of his character as a Nazi. Was not the detached perspective toward his own part in the Final Solution suggested to him early in his career by the fearful prospect shared by Nazi activists of one day being brought to trial? Detachment and "correctness" constituted his anticipatory defense and made up the "legal personality" that the Nazi would present before the bar. "He always told me," testified his friend Dieter Wisliceny, long before Eichmann was caught, "that the most important thing was to be covered at all times by one's superiors. He shunned all personal responsibility and took care to shelter behind his superiors . . . and to inveigle them into accepting liability for all his actions." This Nazi conducted his life of public villainy along the lines of the plea he would make years later in the Jerusalem courtroom. He was an actor whose personality was rigorously fused into the role he had chosen to play. In William Shirer's account of Hitler's moves until his assault on Poland, the Führer's entire strategy pivots on preparing points of retreat and disavowal should the policeman's club rap on the door. In Israel, as earlier in the Weimar Republic, law itself was confounded by a new problem: *that of dealing with a defendant who understands that the basis of Western legal theory is the free act, and who as part of his preparation for his crimes is prepared to deny his freedom.* According to Nazi "modernism," free action is a superstition promulgated by Christian-liberal ideology. The individual who surrenders himself to direction by a corporate political person, such as the National Socialist Party, has recognized that his highest possibility lies in serving the future as a unit of historical energy. A person thus possessed by an agency of history is, by definition, absolved of individual responsibility, and this was made explicit in the Nazi principle of obedience to superiors. Hence a court that presumes to judge a Party member as if he were an individual is engaged not in administering justice but in enforcing its own ideology.

One of the extreme distortions of the Eichmann Trial was that it presented to the world only the courtroom identity of the Party member obeying orders which Eichmann had created over the years for just such a courtroom situation, and which he had refined to the utmost in his long months of imprisonment. The vaunting ego he had disclosed in Argentina to the Dutch journalist Sasser was kept off the stage. So, too, the psychological condition that directly contributed to making the Nazi murder program humanly possible: the waves of collective afflatus that carried Nazis and Germans of all classes from peak to peak of brutal arrogance after Hitler had begun his triumphal march across Europe. Here again the "Chorus" supplied a correction to the trial—after hours of cross-examination in which Eichmann upheld his carefully constructed image of himself as the little clerk checking his memos, a voice from the gallery cried, "But you should have seen him in his SS uniform!"

To Eichmann, playing the part of defendant in the Jerusalem courtroom constituted a purgation of conscience that he could obtain in no other way. The longer the trial went on, the farther removed he became from the reality of his acts and the more *"unschuldig"* he grew in his own eyes— toward the end he was threatening to wreck the trial by confessing indiscriminately if the prosecutor pressed him too hard on points that did not coincide with the image he chose to project. In court Eichmann no longer had to reflect on what he had done. He had only to strengthen the defense made available to him by Western legal tradition, that of having acted within an unbreakable chain of causes or under the direction of a superior will.

The trial was held in order to tell the story of the Jews of Europe. But Eichmann passionately desired to tell *his* story —we know that in 1956, no longer able to endure his incognito, he recounted at length the tale of his life to a stranger he met in a Buenos Aires bar. One may conjecture that being captured by the Israelis was to Eichmann a mixed misfortune. True, his life was put in danger; in return he was given the opportunity to become one of the most memorable figures of this century. What could have meant more to this *"kleiner mann"* who, above all else, found his anonymity intolerable?

Also, what better moment could have been chosen for Eichmann? Had he been brought to the dock at Nuremberg, he would have been overshadowed by scores of offenders far above him in rank and interest: Reich marshals, propagandists, diplomats, slave-labor industrialists—gentlemen who spoke in much the same style as Eichmann and even at times looked like him. In my files, for instance, I find a clipping from *The New York Times* dated January 4, 1946, which contains a photograph of a Major General of Police named Otto Ohlendorf testifying before a War Crimes court. Allow for the fifteen years between his trial and Eichmann's, and this youthful-looking man with his earphones is as much like Eichmann as two cadets or seminarians would be like each other. As to manner and character, the *Times* supplied the following:

The 90,000 lives that Ohlendorf confessed taking at Adolf Hitler's command seemed to rest easily on his conscience. He talked in a matter-of-fact tone, admitting each mass killing as calmly as if the victims had been cattle or sheep. Yet in appearance he is not particularly brutal or inhuman, looking more like a somewhat humorless shoe salesman one might meet anywhere. . . . Ohlendorf described the manner in which Jews were rounded up and killed as a man might describe an ordinary business transaction.

When the world had major generals like this to observe it would have paid scant attention to a mere lieutenant colonel.

By 1961, however, the star performers of Nazi frightfulness had vanished, while mankind, after a decade and a half of respite, was prepared to endure another review of the past. Best of all for Eichmann, he was to be tried in Israel— for only among Jews was he first in importance and certain of recognition in the full scope of his former power.

Eichmann's outlook for immortality would, however, be imperiled if the prosecutor were to rest his case after establishing Eichmann's function as the head of the Department of Jewish Affairs and the steps he had taken to carry out that function. By the precedent of Nuremberg, an accomplice in mass murder may earn a capital sentence, even though his deeds had been performed in obedience to orders. There would not be much satisfaction for Eichmann in a trial that condemned him for his exact part in the complex of decisions and measures constituting the Final Solution. In a case charging him with membership in a murder conspiracy, he would be liable to maximum punishment yet without being relieved of his anonymity.

Eichmann was able to head off such a trial by the confessions in his preliminary examination. Given his willingness to admit his role in the murder operation, it was plain that an indictment restricted to his part in the Final Solution would be met by a plea of guilty—in that event, there would be no trial and the value of Eichmann's capture would be vitiated. There could be a contest and masses of testimony only if Eichmann were charged with personal guilt over and above actions incontestably related to his Gestapo functions. In sum, the condition for a full-scale trial was that Eichmann's personality should be made central to the question of his guilt.

With this kind of accusation of personal evil Eichmann was prepared to cope. Having mounted the world stage, he would now defend himself, like Hitler before him, as the little man, the put-upon "front soldier," the honest victim of misunderstanding and prejudice—specifically, of being nothing more than the "link in the sausage," the "cog in the machine." Seen abstractly—that is, apart from the murder apparatus and the actual bodies which Eichmann had been feeding into it—this was a defense which the contemporary world could thoroughly appreciate. The Nazi mind is nothing if not "modern;" the strength of Hitler's movement lay in its keen grasp of the perversities of present-day experience, and in its cynicism in making use of them. Chief among these perversities is the complacent letting go of self and responsibility by persons functioning in large organizations. Eichmann's defense was designed to appeal to the universal appreciation of the plight of the organization man. Who cannot grasp that one in the middle of a chain of command—a link in the sausage— simply passes down orders he receives from above, without having the power to alter their content or to influence their ultimate effect? Everyone in an organization is in a sense nothing but a "traffic officer," while the directors at the top reach decisions that reflect a collective mind separate from that of each. It is the fictitious being of the corporation that acts, while the human beings in the company are mere tools. And this plea of immunity through the corporation is one that sits well in legal logic; for the corporation, like the government bureau, is the creature of the law itself; it is a "fictitious legal entity," set up to supply immunity to individuals who manipulate its levers. In the business corporation the immunity is restricted to the economic; in the corporate state it is total. And while it is not thinkable that one's business is to dispatch living human shipments to death factories, by analogy with the clean hands of the office man in charge of shipping fish fertilizer or veal carcasses, it *is* thinkable.

With the cog idea Eichmann was able to play the Nazi double game of the servile hero. He was a nobody acting under orders; but this nobody had been able, in order to do his gruesome duty, heroically to conquer the creature in himself, with its sentiments, its weaknesses. Eichmann told how he faltered at the sight of the "fountain of blood," but he added that had he been ordered to do so he would have slain his own father. Thus the "cog" becomes the protagonist of an ethical drama, overcoming in anguish his excess of human feelings. In the end he is, in his own eyes, a noble warrior deserving sympathy and respect for his conflicts and sufferings. In sum, Eichmann's defense exemplified the chicanery of the *protected* elite with which the Nazis allured the leaders of Germany's industry and armed forces —through the Nazi concept of the cog each would be able to avoid his own responsibility for the Nazis, at the same time that he achieved power and distinction through his identification with them.

A cog cannot, of course, be concerned with the suffering inflicted by the machine of which it is a part. Eichmann's defense counsel endeavored to associate him with the literary image of an inquisitor so "abstract" that the screams of the victims could not break through his absorption with his gears and timetables. Such an abstract man, however, is authentic only if he is also indifferent to his personal interests and to his own pain, like the officer of Kafka's *The Penal Colony* who throws himself into the lethal machine out of fidelity to his idea. But what of a "cog" that is ambitious for promotions and infinitely concerned with staying alive? What of this dedicated agent of death who consistently shows so much ardor in prolonging his own existence? The efforts of Eichmann following the end of the war to save his skin destroy any credibility that might attach itself to the image of the dedicated slave of orders from above. He executed those orders because he benefited from executing them—his lust to survive belies any surrender of self to the "machine," any transcendence into impersonality. His behavior after the Nazi collapse demonstrates that, like most of his fellow criminals, he gave himself to the Führer and the Party not as a religious convert gives himself to his cult but as a swindler adopts the discipline of a gang. Eichmann in court personified the fraudulence of Nazi alienation. His enterprising self-defense, in proving that he committed his crimes in expected security, made him personally guilty of the death of each human being he delivered to the executioner.

Eichmann's distortion of the relation between an individual and the organization to which he belongs gave his defense its typical Nazi character. It was a defense that arose from the very heart of the present-day intellectual juggling with responsibility through which the Nazis had arrived at the principle of the all-responsible Führer and the strategy of bureaucratic disavowal. Through Hitler, a Party and a nation of innocents were created by drawing everyone into the corporation (everyone, that is, who was to be allowed to survive). Except for Hitler himself, each of these corporate limbs or organization men could claim before the bar of liberal jurisprudence that as a man he was something other than his actions and opposed to them. In contrast to the necessity imposed upon his behavior by the organization,* his freedom was private, inward and intangible, and he would demand that his inner qualities be taken into account as the real he.

Thus to convict Eichmann *totally*, Prosecutor Hausner strove to "restore," as a *New York Times* headline put it, "the arch-killer," to prove Eichmann subjectively an enemy of the Jews, one animated by "bottomless hatred" and "murderous fury," and still devoid of remorse;† while Judge Landau asked Dr. Servatius during the latter's summation: "Do we have anything in the testimony of the accused . . . which shows that he revolted internally against the extermination orders?" But suppose he had "revolted internally" while still continuing to send Jews to the ovens? He did revolt, Dr. Servatius replied, but he was powerless to make his objections manifest. So the issue seemed unresolved—in contrast to the electrical monopoly cases in which the U.S. Federal judge indignantly cast

---

* It will be recalled that one of the dramatic moments of the trial came when Eichmann stepped out of his glass cage to defend himself with—an organization chart.

† Hausner's complaint in his summation that Eichmann showed no remorse indicated that the prosecutor either failed or refused to understand Eichmann's defense: since, according to it no harm had emanated from Eichmann as a person, but only passed through him as a "link," he had nothing to regret, except perhaps having been imposed upon by the Nazi "error."

aside evidence regarding the personal good character of the defendants, as well as the defense of orders from above. For unless the law judges according to the actions of the defendant, it risks losing itself in the metaphysics of doing versus being. In the Eichmann Trial, perhaps out of excessive sensitivity to the coercion of individuals by impersonal forces, what the defendant had *not* done was allowed to become part of the proceedings, as Hitler had been allowed by the democratic world to talk about not invading Czechoslovakia after he had delivered his ultimatum. But except for being the executive in charge of the Gestapo's Jew-killing department—how careful he was to distinguish the responsibility of this department from that of the Wehrmacht and the Foreign Office!—Eichmann was "a man like everyone else."

By the conditions of his trial, Eichmann had to be allowed to compete with the survivors in their telling of the story of the Jews of Europe. He had to be allowed his defense, deceitful, absurd and outrageous as it was. The issue of his subjective guilt was, however, a distraction that ought to have been reduced to a minimum. Why should this self-styled nobody who had crushed into silence so many of the subtlest and most humane intellects of Europe have been permitted to elaborate on each trait of his character, each twist of his career, his opinions on all sorts of matters, including Kant's categorical imperative, and his conception of himself as Pontius Pilate and as an "idealist" and a "romantic," his reaction to his wife's reading the Bible, his drinking of mare's milk and *schnapps?* One question would have sufficed to complete the formulation of his culpability: "Weren't you the head of Sec. IV B4 of RSHA charged with the extermination of the Jews of Europe and did you not carry out the function assigned to you to the best of your ability?" Any intimation that one could be *more* guilty than Eichmann after his admission that "I knew that some of the Jews would be exterminated" revealed an intrinsic confusion of values. Regardless of the verdict, the trial should have affirmed in the most positive terms that absolutely nothing could weigh a hairbreadth in the guilt of one who had performed with efficiency and zeal the job of deliberately sending innocent men, women and children to be tortured, shot and gassed.

Unfortunately, the Israeli Attorney General accepted with the zeal of a courtroom David the challenge of Eichmann to prove his inner viciousness as well as the criminality of his deeds. The world looked to the testimony of Eichmann not for an image of the Fiend but for a clearer and more detailed delineation of the evolution of the Nazi murder plan out of programs of discrimination and expulsion, for information on where the action of the Final Solution began and what each category of its executants had added to it in practice. Instead of light on these matters, it got Eichmann's contest with the prosecutor, as Mr. Hausner strove by cross-examination (in which shouts of "liar" and heavy sarcasm were met by sour rage) to "break down" the defendant as in a case of manslaughter or burglary. For twenty-five days the stage was surrendered to this tournament. In the interval the anguish of Auschwitz and Maidanek was forced into the background. Yet in the end the Attorney General, for all his oratory about Eichmann's murdering with "fervor and insatiable lust," was compelled to fall back on the irrefutable charge of his being "involved in a conspiracy to commit crimes against the Jewish people and against humanity . . . and occupying a central position in this conspiracy in its executive stage."

While the story of the mass victim had been shredded into bits by courtroom procedure, the defense was able from first to last to maintain a single, continuing impression: that of the embattled prisoner parrying endless questions and confrontations with itemized explanations of his lack of responsibility. By the time the cross-examination was over, each molecule of the enormous crime had been funneled through Eichmann into a void. Even his style of speech had been used to veil the atrocious reality which the trial had attempted to communicate: "He seemed," wrote *The New York Times*, "to be avoiding wherever possible the use of words like Jews, death, concentration camps. His testimony was shot through with mention of superior orders, and it was immersed in the special jargon of bureaucracy." Eichmann's weeks on the stand had the effect not of breaking him down but of breaking down in the mind of the world audience the outlines, traced with such difficulty, of a conspiracy of murderous men and mingling it into an *impersonal process*. Not only was the form of events lost but even their chronology. "Mr. Hausner," Presiding Judge Landau complained at one point, "we discussed Holland and France last week and now we have come back to them again."

Thus there was presented in Jerusalem an indispensable account of the tragedy of the Jews in this era—but it was an account marred in the telling and needing to be retold and interpreted again and again.

10

Missing Persons

"Alienation," a term once confined to philosophy, law, psychiatry and advanced literary criticism, has entered the common vocabulary. Newspaper columns refer without quotes or elucidation to the alienation of the slum dweller, the drug addict, the vanguard poet; popular fiction writers rely on readers to recognize the symptoms of alienation as a motive for adultery or murder. Alienage, or strangeness, is understood to be not only a condition (as of foreigners) but a process (as of losing oneself in a vocational routine). As they say in the fund-raising drives of health organizations, it can happen to anyone.

The term is a tricky one—as currently used, "alienation" has at least two meanings that are often unrelated and at times even opposed. It can mean estrangement of a person *from* society or his estrangement from himself *through* society. The delinquent is estranged but so too is the organization man.

Before the war, American literature dealt mainly with alienation of the first type, separation from society brought about either by the person's own choice (his awakening as a poet or lover) or by discrimination or hard luck (minorities, Okies). A popular motif in the novels of the twenties (e.g., Floyd Dell) was the conformist-seeming husband or wife who goes out to get the morning paper and sets off without warning in search of a more authentic existence. With regard to society this protagonist became a missing person, a personification of the outsider. But in regard to himself, he was the opposite: one who had conquered the spell of social convention and had come to recognize what he himself was like.

The much-discussed estrangement of the artist and intellectual is of the same order as that of the defector from domestic routine. He removes himself from his neighbors and their beliefs in order to gain access to his own sensibility. In turn, artistic alienation parallels that of the unassimilated immigrant and excluded black. All these "strangers" live at a distance from society, but this is compensated for by closer ties among themselves, as in Genet's love colonies of jailbirds. The resemblance between the alienation of intellectuals and that of minorities has prompted a critic of Irish descent to identify himself as a Jew, a Jewish novelist to dub himself a "white Negro," and a female novelist-critic to attach herself to a band of homosexual painters.

Quite different from the alienation of the self-exiled vanguardist or the excluded foreigner or black is the alienation of the good citizen psychologically missing in the performance of his duties. He is *in* society, but his separation is all the more painful for being owing to invisible causes. The estrangement of the Bohemian is balanced by the identity he establishes through his group; together with the delinquent, the immigrant or the mountain dweller, he has his place in a "subculture." There is, however, nothing that makes up for the estrangement of the salesman, the factory hand, the computer operator, the corporation executive—in a word, the contemporary citizen. His isolation is not from society but from himself, and this inner vacuum puts him at a distance not only from those he greets every day but even from the things in his living room. In all outer respects normal, he lives in a jelly of unreality that differs only in density from that which surrounds the schizophrenic or the opium eater. Here the line of estrangement is drawn not around the individual but directly through his center. The psychically alienated citizen is entirely present in the flesh, but some undefined power has sequestered him and turned him into something other than a human being—Ionesco's rhinoceros perhaps, or Beckett's bag o' bones in a trash can. Nor is his apartness remediable by integration through rehabilitation programs that affect other outsiders, for example, removal of restrictions on housing, jobs or clubs. If the inner division of the citizen is to be healed, it can only be through drastic alteration both of his inner being and of his mode of existence. For his trouble arose out of his performance of the very functions which unite him with society and to which he owes his identity and his status. He is trapped outside of his existence by the web of routines that binds him to his community, his family, his own values.

In sum, estranged through his actions, including the most necessary and praiseworthy, the citizen is the victim of a fundamental irony of the human condition. Modern alienation of this sort is a phase of that otherness which has been a theme of religion, drama, philosophy and myth throughout the history of mankind. As Marx put it, the difference between oneself as a person and as a member of society "is not a conceptual difference but an historical fact."

Alienation as a metaphysical malady discovered in the common man has since the fifties come to be more discussed than the alienation of the social outsider—even the most convinced black integrationist has had to face the issue that victory meant winning the privilege of being infected with the alienation of the whites. The threat of loss of self through participating in the economic, social and cultural processes of our mass society has brought Americans closer to ultimate questions than at any time since the Bible lay open on the parlor table. Writings interpreting contemporary culture in terms of alienation have reached flood proportions in fiction, sociology, psychiatry, philosophy, history. The man without a face, once a character of the comic strip and science fiction, has taken up his habitation in the factory, the office, the consultation room and the lecture hall. Robotization has been found lurking both as cause and effect behind every facet of modern life, from supermarket packaging to totalitarian atrocities. As the dominant convention in the theater and the novel, the concept of the slipped ego of modern man has become a powerful modulator of moral attitudes. Opinion in support of Hannah Arendt's *Eichmann in Jerusalem* almost invariably demanded acknowledgment that in our time men did become, as Eichmann averred, "cogs in the machine," so that the actor stood apart from his actions as a detached and even dissenting observer. Given the two meanings of alienation, one feared that Eichmann's estrangement might be equated with that of German refugees.

The social misery of the contemporary individual arises from the quality of the roles available to him; for example, the despair of today's university student consists in facing a life confined to the corporation, the government agency, the campus. In the organized society the citizen feels hemmed in and propelled by external forces. It is a mistake, however, to conceive him as tormented by social roles in general; except in extreme situations—love, the threat of death—the opposition between self and social mask seems abstract and illusory. For the individual to fit himself into a part appears not only to be unavoidable but highly desirable; most of the satisfactions of life and its meanings arise from what the individual does in the social context. His effort is not to avoid assuming a role but to guarantee that his part shall be a proper one. The force of ambition testifies to the superior worth placed on one role versus another; and revolutions have been fought to make "careers open to talent."

To condemn all social roles as infected with the void, as Tolstoy did in *The Death of Ivan Ilych* (making an exception of the peasant), and as is often done in present-day radical manifestos, is to call for nothing less than the overthrow of civilized society. It is to criticize human life from the point of view of the saint or mystic—to raise the banner of permanent revolution. Marx was aware of this implication when, in analyzing the alienating labor of the modern factory worker, he condemned as well all conditions by which man had been estranged throughout history. "Scientific" socialism undertook to eliminate the otherness in man responsible for nature demons and idols, fetishes and spectres (what can be more alienated than a ghost?). To cure alienation in this sense, Marx knew, required passing beyond history into "the revolution in permanence"—a condition of uplifted primitivism.

But even if work were to become completely free and all social roles were to become fluid, metaphysical alienation would not be overcome. The estrangement of Socrates, Hamlet or Kierkegaard is the effect not of common processes but of their own choice, and its substance is the unique activity of a single individual. Its content is not the inadequacy of society but voluntary immersion in dissolution and death.

Far from freeing the individual, the Utopian ideal of healing the metaphysical division in man through transforming the meaning of work threatens him with enslavement. Conceiving the individual's social function as the ground of his identity can, as with Eichmann, serve to exalt a criminal occupation. It can also, as in the Soviet Union, provide the theoretical justification for hunting down the nonconformist as a parasite or a madman.

In stable periods hankerings after wholeness may be an expression of poetic nostalgia—for the South Sea Islands before the White Devil arrived; for the "Medieval Synthesis"; for the Florence of the Medicis—and keep alive noble ideals. In times of crisis, however, the mirage of surmounting the split between self and role (e.g., through total identification with the Party or leader) as a way of dealing with specific social ills (e.g., the anonymity of routine jobs) can give rise to demonic rituals. All twentieth-century totalitarian movements have sold themselves to the masses as antidotes to alienation. All have taken an oath to eliminate the gap between the individual and society, and between public self and private self. All have marketed a synthetic version of tragic catharsis.

Masses who have faced death on the battlefield or in air raids, and have experienced the dissolution of accustomed forms, become susceptible to moods of emptiness and detachment in which no action seems valid unless it promises a total alteration of life. Yet no common program can compensate an individual for the collapse of the "I" which he had previously recognized as himself. One of the great lessons of the failed revolutions of the twentieth century is that ultimate problems of the self cannot be solved by political means. The attack on alienation as an evil peculiar to capitalism, democracy, the industrial age or mass society has led instead to a cynical radicalism in which the non-person is taken for granted as the disposable component of a manipulated society. Or it has led to literary despair and sham profundity that denies the possibility of individual or collective action—in current writings it is often difficult to distinguish alienation from dyspepsia.

Alienation is neither a reflex to modern crowds and computers nor is it a disease for which the future will supply a vaccine. Every act of creation involves a degree of otherness, and the right of the person to alienate himself from himself and from society—as in the institution of the Nazarite in the Old Testament or in the name-changing rituals of the Greek cults—is the most exalted and indispensable of privileges.

Notes and
Acknowledgments

In arranging these pieces, I have at times altered their chronological order to provide intervals of relief between the more difficult theoretical expositions. The opening chapter was written last, for a magazine planned by the director of the Lincoln Center theater, which, however, never appeared—it is the only piece in the collection not previously published. The earliest of the essays, "The Riddles of Oedipus," first appeared as "Notes on Identity" in the American surrealist periodical *View* in 1946 and was reprinted in a revised version many years later in *The Tulane Drama Review* at the instigation of Eric Bentley, who remembered the article and wanted it to come to light again in the context of the theater.

The theme of the actor in search of his non-performable self and of his real situation was resumed a year later in "The Stages," published in the art-literary magazine *Possibilities* in 1947 and shortly thereafter in *Les Temps Modernes* under the inspired title of "Du Jeu au Je"—a formulation which I appreciatively re-echoed some two decades later in calling my review of Sartre's *The Words* "From Playacting to Self." Sartre's connection with "The Stages" had been cemented by the fact that he had found in it motives for his play *Les Mains Sales* (*Red Gloves*)— but my discussion of *Hamlet* could scarcely be identified with Existentialism, since it followed up on a portion of an essay published more than a decade before the Existentialist movement began.*

"The Pathos of the Proletariat," first printed in *The Kenyon Review* in 1949, and subsequently in *Les Temps Modernes*, was the second of two essays on the drama of modern history as conceived by Marx—a drama in which individual identity and action were replaced by collective actors formed out of historical processes and myths. In the United States, Marx's philosophy had by the end of the forties lost its prestige in intellectual circles, whose ritual radicalism had given way to a dutiful anti-Communism that extended all the way to chauvinism and collaboration with government investigative agencies. I continued, however, to see in Marx's writings a grand scaffold on which current political, social and cultural phenomena appear to interact in a significant way. At the same time, I saw with increasing clarity that Marx's critical-dramatic vision of history, profound and relevant as it was, terminated in a fantasy: the triumph of a non-existent collective actor, the proletariat. At bottom Marx erred, it seemed to me, in assuming that the alienation of individuals and the ancient drama of self-recognition would be resolved through revolutionizing the social conditions of work. As a direct result of this seemingly abstruse theoretical flaw in dialectical materialism, individuals in societies ruled by Marxism have come to be considered mere reflexes of their

* "Character Change and the Drama," *The Symposium*, 1932; collected in *The Tradition of the New* (New York: Horizon Press, 1959).

social roles, and expressions of their inner uncertainties and conflicts have been outlawed—in a word, the individual has been outlawed and his development driven underground.

"Criticism-Action," written as a chapter of the anthology on world thinkers, *Les Philosophes Célèbres,* edited by Maurice Merleau-Ponty, Professor of Philosophy at the Collège de France (the English original was published in *Dissent* in 1956), reiterates, unavoidably, some of the points in "The Pathos of the Proletariat." But the perspective of the new piece is different—it focuses more closely on current conditions—and things are stated differently. I therefore thought it preferable to present it intact rather than attempt to incorporate it into the earlier essay. Also, a certain amount of circling about should be useful in making this terrain more familiar.

The chapter on Eichmann, "Guilt to the Vanishing Point," was written during the course of the trial in Jerusalem and published in *Commentary* in November, 1961. It endeavored to contrast the drama of the victims of the Nazi slaughter and its survivors with the version of it staged under the limitations of Israeli courtroom procedure; and it analyzed Eichmann as an actor consciously striving to confine his guilt to the role he claimed had been imposed upon him by the Nazi Party, while he kept his "true self" apart from his crimes and, thus, beyond the reach of personal responsibility.

A similar splitting of self from public performance, though of course in a completely different moral setting, is discussed in the chapter on Sartre's *The Words,* originally published in *The New Yorker* in 1968. "Actor in History" appeared as "Malraux and His Critics" in the *Art News Annual* of 1966.

Another piece first published in *The New Yorker* is the

chapter on Dostoyevsky's *The Idiot,* "A Psychological Case," which was commissioned as the introduction to a new translation of the novel issued by The New American Library in 1969. I am especially pleased to include in the present context Dostoyevsky's conception of modern individuals as mimics of fictional types, of their incapacity to act, and of the ultimately aesthetic character of modern values.

A version of the chapter on alienation, "Missing Persons," was prepared for the Book Section of the Sunday *New York Times* and appeared there in 1963. Estrangement seems an appropriate subject with which to conclude these speculations concerning the act and the actor.

Index

Abstract art, 168

Act: Valéry quoted on, 3; whole acts as belonging to epochs of myth, 4; with no beginning or end, in world of nature, 4; of an individual, character of, 4; melding of human act into events, 4–5; the human act as outstanding riddle of 20th century, 6; indeterminacy of, in art and social relations, 6; "gratuitous" act, purged of motive, 6–7; and duration of the creative act, 10; status of, in 20th century drama, 11–12

Action painting, 6, 9

Activism of Lenin, 148

Albee, Edward, 11

Alienation, 198; two meanings of term, 198; as a metaphysical malady, 201, 202–03; totalitarian movements sold as antidotes to, 203; as an inherent right of the individual, 204. *See also* Estrangement

American, the: as Europe's barbarian, 27; and action, 28, 31; proletariat as embodiment of attributes of, 29; as representative of the modern, 29–30, 31

Amerika (Kafka), 7

Anarchists, 153

Anonymity: Eichmann's escape from, 189–91; of routine jobs, 203

Anti-Semitism: Eichmann Trial as warning of dangers of, 176–80; Eichmann's denial of personal feelings of, 176–77; and Nazism, 177–80

Arendt, Hannah, 201

Aristotle, ix, xii, xviii

Art: intuition of indeterminacy of the act as underlying factor in, 6; and duration of creative act, 10

Art criticism of Malraux, 167–69

Artists, alienation of, 199

Authority, x

Bacon, xv

Balzac, Honoré de, 147

Baudelaire, Charles Pierre, 125

Beckett, Samuel, 8, 9, 12, 200

Being and Nothingness (Sartre), 126

Ben-Gurion, David, 172, 176

Bernstein, Eduard, 148

Blake, William, 124

Blanchot, Maurice, 155, 158

Bolshevism, 44*n.*, 53, 54, 161, 163, 165, 175

Boredom of routine jobs, 203

Bourgeoisie, 18, 21, 25, 38, 40, 137, 147

Bouvard et Pécuchet (Flaubert), 28*n.*

Brecht, Bertolt, 12, 148

Brothers Karamazov, The (Dostoyevsky), 116

Camden's Eyes (Wright), 7

Camus, Albert, 107

Change, x

Capital (Marx), 16, 17, 20, 35, 51, 137, 138

Capitalism, 17, 21, 28, 34, 36, 43, 51, 54, 137–38, 139, 141, 143, 146; collapse of, xviii

Castle, The (Kafka), 7

Chiang Yee, xx
Chiaramonte, Nicola, 157–58, 161, 164, 166
Chinese Revolution, 152, 159, 161
Chorus in Greek theater, 125, 185; simulation in outcries at Eichmann Trial, 185, 188
Civil War in France, The (Marx), 22, 40, 149
Class: Marx on, 14, 16–20; relation of individual to, 14–15, 54, 136, 142; as personification, 17–20, 56; classes as makers of history, 22, 57; as historical actor, 22–23; class identity of laboring masses, 64–65; evolution of class struggles, 139; displacement of, by leaders of the Party, 148–49. *See also* Proletariat; Working class
Class Struggles in France, The (Marx), 19, 22, 44
"Cog in the machine": Eichmann's defense, 5, 192–94, 197; modern man as, 201
Collectivization of production, 150
Communism, 14, 29, 33, 34, 36, 42, 52, 138, 144, 147–48 154, 156, 161, 163
Communist Manifesto, The (Marx and Engels), 20, 21, 25, 51, 144
Community, the, 33–35, 52, 56, 136
Computer operator, estrangement from himself, 200
Conquerors, The (Malraux), 152–53, 155, 156, 161, 162
Constant, the, x
Contemporary citizen: estrangement from himself, 200; quality of roles available to, 201–02
Corporation executive, estrangement from himself, 200
Counterfeiters, The (Gide), 7
Creative act by man, 9, 10
Creative elite, theories of, 9
Crime, alienation as motive for, 198
Crime and Punishment (Dostoyevsky), 5, 7, 59, 111, 116, 117
Criticism: and revolution as complementary, 138, 140–41, 144; as an action, for Marx, 140, 145
"Crusade" of De Gaulle, 25n.
Cubism, 168

Darkness at Noon (Koestler), 161

Days of Wrath (Malraux), 156, 165
Death of Ivan Ilych, The (Tolstoy), 132, 202
Defector from domestic routine, estrangement of, 199
De Gaulle, Charles, 25n., 157, 159, 169
De-individualization of Industrial Man, 5, 151
Delinquent, estrangement of, 198, 199
Dell, Floyd, 199
Descartes, René, 128
Determinism, 4, 6, 162, 168
Dewey, John, 94
Diary of a Writer, The (Dostoyevsky), 123
Diderot, Denis, 42
Dostoyevsky, Feodor, xix, 5, 7, 72–73, 104–25, 158
Drama: and traditional imitation of action in, 11; status of the act in 20th century drama, 11–12; and theater of the non-act, 12; and self-knowledge of the hero, 58–59; "Know thyself" as link between philosophy and, 65
Drug addict, alienation of, 198

East, traditions of the, xiv
Eichmann, Adolph, 5, 170–97; trial in terms of its moral and historical effects, 171–72; trial as "political case," 172–75; distortions of trial, 173, 188; retelling at trial of anguish of Jews at hands of Nazis, 174–75, 184; trial as warning of dangers of anti-Semitism, 176–80; trial as representing recovery of Jews from shock of Nazi outrages, 180–81; as living protagonist for Nazi crimes against the Jews, 182 –83; trial as reenactment of horrors of story of the Jews, 183–84, 197; refusal to assume personal responsibility for deeds, 184, 187–89, 191, 195–97; "legal personality" presented by, at trial, 187–89; and escape from anonymity, 189–91; "cog in the machine" defense, 192 –94, 197, 201; lack of remorse, 194; testimony of, at his trial, 195 –97

Othello, 59

Party, the: as collective "I" of proletariat, 47; ideology and discipline of, 47–48, 51; and working class, 48, 52, 55, 56; displacement of the class by leaders of, 148–49
Past, abandonment of, by proletarian revolution, 23–24, 28, 37
Perception, humanistic, xvi
Pererspectives in Humanism, ix
Philosophy: "Know thyself" as link between drama and, 65; and problem of individual identity, 65–73; modern action philosophy, 69; despair of the dramatic philosopher, 70–71
Pirandello, Luigi, 12
Play acting, Sartre's development to self from, 126–34
Playing one's part well, as primary human obligation, 3–4
Political economy of Marx, 18–19, 135
Politics: and struggle between advocates of mass spontaneity and centralized direction, 10; Marxian, 41–42, 51–55, 144; conflict in Marxism between metaphysics and, 52–53
Pollock, Jackson, 168
Power, x
Prejudice, antihumanist, xvi
Program, socialist, xviii
Proletariat: pathos of, 14–57; as hero of Marx's drama of history, 14–15, 23, 41; as revolutionary, 18, 21, 23–24, 28, 36, 37, 39–40, 41, 44, 45, 46; abandonment of past by revolution of, 23–24, 28, 37; as modern invention, 24–29, 30–31; "Americanizing" of, 32; reality-inspired "I" of, 36; conversion of, from a personification into actor, 38; historical consciousness of, 39, 40, 41, 43–45, 46–47, 51, 52, 53; collective "I" of, becomes the Party, 47. *See also* Working class
Proust, Marcel, 133
Pseudonyms, use by authors, 67–68
Psychoanalysis, 58, 60, 63–64, 72

Radicalism, proletarian, 21
Rationalism, 42, 112

Raw Youth, A (Dostoyevsky), 7, 73
Realism of Dostoyevsky, 111, 121, 124
Reitlinger, Gerald, 181
Revenge, as motive for action, 85
Revisionist socialism of Bernstein, 148
Revolution: socialist, 15, 38, 51, 52, 144; proletarian, 18, 21, 23–24, 28, 36, 37, 39–40, 41, 44, 45, 46; bourgeois, 18, 37, 40; in permanence, 26, 40, 50, 51, 143, 202; technological, 35; of 1848, 44, 45–46; and criticism as complementary, 138, 140–41, 144; Bolshevik, 165
Rhetorical Hero, The (Righter), 159–60
Rhinoceros, The (Ionesco), 130, 200
Righter, William, 159–60, 164, 166
Rilke, Rainer Maria, 27, 28
Rimbaud, Arthur, 26, 27, 35, 40
Robotization, and psychical alienation, 201
Routine jobs, boredom and anonymity of, 203
Russia and the Russians, as represented by Dostoyevsky in *The Idiot,* 108–09, 112, 123

Salesman, estrangement from himself, 200
Salvation: Christian promise of, 72; *The Idiot* as Dostoyevsky's book of, 107, 117; Sartre's urge toward, 131–32
Sartre, Jean-Paul, 126–34
Science, xv; pre-analytic data of, xv; objectivity of, xx
Scientist, xiv
Self: mass transformation of, as pathos of socialist movement, 36; incommunicability of, 68; Sartre's development from play acting to, 126–34; threat of loss of, through processes of our mass society, 201; opposition between social mask and, 202; and hankerings after wholeness, 203; split between role and, 203; problems of, not solvable by political means, 204
Shirer, William, 187
Slumdweller, alienation of, 198
Social class. *See* Class

Socialism, 19–20, 20, 33, 36, 41, 42, 47, 52, 56, 144, 146, 148; "scientific," 42, 202
Social outsider, alienation of, 201
Social relations, intuition of indeterminacy of the act as underlying factor in, 6
Sorel, Georges, 51, 57
Spanish Civil War, Loyalist cause in, 155, 156, 161, 162, 164
Spengler, Oswald, 168
Stalin, Joseph, 5, 156,162,175
Stalin-Hitler Pact, 163
Story of a Cheat (Guitry), 131
Stranger, The (Camus), 107
Studies, historical, xii
Symbol, xx

Temptation of the West (Malraux), 156, 158
Terrorism, Marxian, 55
Tolstoy, Leo, 132–33, 202
Totalitarianism, 150, 201, 203
Tradition, Western, xiv
Trotsky, Leon, 29, 42, 44*n.*, 152, 153, 155, 161, 164

Ulysses (Joyce), 8
Unity, xvii
University students of today, despair of, 201–02

Utopians, 41*n.*, 51, 141, 203

Valéry, Paul, 3, 12–13
Vocational routine, losing oneself in, 198
Voltaire, 42

Wage labor. *See* Working class
Waiting for Godot (Beckett), 8–9
Walnut Trees of Altenburg, The (Malraux), 158
Wansee Conference (1942), 178
Weiss, Peter, 10–11, 12
What Is to Be Done? (Lenin), 53*n.*
Williams, Tennessee, 11
Wilson, Edmund, 155
Wisliceny, Dieter, 187
Words, The (Sartre), 126–34
Working class: as revolutionary, 19, 21, 32, 39–40, 56, 143; as personification of wage labor, 23–24, 56; anguish of, 36; positive existence of, only through collective action of its members, 36; and the Party, 47, 48, 52, 55, 56; centering of Marx's historical materialism on future victory of, 140–41; revolutionary activity as materialist criticism of, 144. *See also* Proletariat
Wright, Austin, 7